26 Short Plays for Classro

Take A Quick Bow!

By Pamela Marx
Illustrated by Tom James

Good Year Books
An Imprint of Addison-Wesley Educational Publishers, Inc.

To Mark

and to Megan, Holly, Ryan, Chris, and Michael

Acknowledgments

My grateful appreciation goes to the following people for their help in testing plays, making suggestions, giving and testing activity ideas, and/or providing reading resource suggestions: the students of Dahlia Heights School, Pamela Olson, Marlene Culver, Margaret Villarreal, Eileen Hatrick, Melodie Conrad, Susan Sides, Rhonda Heth, Lisa Skylar, Holly Goldstein, Megan Goldstein, Debbie Mansfield, Debbie Vodhanel, Martha Gustafson, and Mark Goldstein.

Good Year Books

are available for most basic curriculum subjects plus many enrichment areas. For more Good Year Books, contact your local bookseller or educational dealer. For a complete catalog with information about other Good Year Books, please write:

Good Year Books

1900 East Lake Avenue

Glenview, IL 60025

Book Design: Grenier Design Associates

Text Copyright © 1997 Pamela Marx.

Illustrations Copyright © 1997 Addison-Wesley Educational Publishers, Inc.

All Rights Reserved.

Printed in the United States of America.

ISBN 0-673-36316-3

3 4 5 6 7 8 9 - MH - 04 03 02 01 00 99 98

TABLE OF CONTENTS

INTRODUCTION: HOW TO USE THIS BOOK VII

III

TABLE OF CONTENTS

V

TAKE A QUICK BOW!

VI

INTRODUCTION:
HOW TO USE THIS BOOK

This book contains 26 short performance vehicles appropriate for children in grades 2–4. Most are easy-to-stage plays, while several are choral speaking performance pieces. Most of the plays have a linear structure that allows groups of actors to enter and leave the stage one after another, making staging easy and straightforward even in the most adverse settings (for example, front of classroom as stage). While the plays provide a performance structure, there is room in some plays for students to write certain lines themselves. As such the plays provide an opportunity not only for memorization and performance, but for creative thinking and some original script writing within a structured framework.

The book organizes the plays by content areas. These include seasons; winter holidays; international folklore (suitable for exploring cultural diversity, as well as celebrating holidays of different countries and ethnicities, such as Chinese New Year ("The Magic Pears"), Cinco de Mayo ("Tale of the Duendes"), and St. Patrick's Day (The Children and the Leprechauns' Gold"); traditions and history of the United States (suitable for Fourth of July, Flag Day, Presidents' Day and Memorial Day); environmental issues; the arts (suitable for learning about art, sculpture, poetry, and, by reference to the seasonal plays, music); equality and brotherhood (suitable for Black History or Women's History Months,

Martin Luther King, Jr.'s, birthday, United Nations Day or peace-themed events); and the sciences (providing plays that let children tell about science facts they are learning in class, as well as complete plays on weather and technology—specifically, simple machines). With such diversity in subject matter, teachers and other play directors should be able to find an appropriate play for any particular school or community event.

Although some of the subject matter may seem advanced for the younger grades, it is never too early to expose children to history, art, literature, and so on, in this playful way. In later years children will study these areas further and will benefit by having this frame of reference.

The performance pieces in this book are simple enough to prepare for performance in four or five rehearsals over a one- or two-week period. Their duration is from three to four minutes for the shorter pieces to nine to twelve minutes for the longer plays. As such, they are quite usable as part of a larger assembly format in which many classes participate. Play directors who choose to use them for stand-alone performances may couple a play with other material for a longer performance. The "Perform It" section following the script text of each play includes ideas for oral speaking, song, and dance segments that may be performed in conjunction with each play.

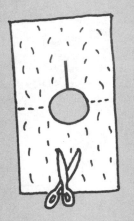

Because the speaking experience is important for each child, the plays have thirty speaking parts. Some actor roles have more than one line. Most have only one. Pair students with roles according to their ability to handle multiple lines or slightly more complex parts. Where multiple lines exist, they are often quite short or very repetitive. In those plays with longer individual parts, encourage children to change their lines as necessary to make them easier to say, as long as the meaning remains substantially the same.

Designed to be flexible, these plays can be shortened or lengthened with relative ease to fit individual needs. Although there are thirty speaking parts, you can easily adapt the plays for less or more children by deleting or adding lines. In addition, some of the children can double up on lines as appropriate. Teachers with more than thirty students should feel free to share lines between students (especially longer, multi-sentence lines), and to add script lines as needed. As the children become familiar with the play, even young children can find ways to add lines.

The plays require only minimal costuming and scenery for the simple reason that time and money are often limited. Auxiliary matters such as costumes and props should not serve as stumbling blocks to giving children the valuable experiences play production offers. The italicized stage direction information in the script text discusses appropriate props. The "Perform It" section, found on the "Teacher's Notes" pages following each play, includes costume

suggestions. If none are given, students should wear white shirts and black pants or skirts as the basic stage clothing ensemble. With this "standard black and white stage clothing" as a starting point, referred to in the "Perform It" sections throughout the book, one can add simple accessories such as sashes and aprons to suggest a variety of characters and costume looks.

Another costuming idea referenced in the "Perform It" sections is the no-sew tunic. A no-sew tunic (see illustration at left) is simply a length of fabric approximately eighteen to twenty-two inches wide and sixty inches long (which can be belted at the waist, if appropriate). Cut a head hole and slit so that the child can slip it on over his or her head. This tunic concept can serve as the costuming effect for a wide variety of parts, depending upon the fabric used and the precise shape of the edges of the tunic.

Each play is constructed in an easy-to-follow fashion and is followed by helpful "Teacher's Notes." Each play starts with a list of characters and a note about the setting and then is followed by script text that includes stage direction and prop/scenery ideas. Following each play are the "Teacher's Notes" that are divided into the following sections for your convenience.

PERFORM IT

This section provides simple costume ideas for each play's characters, such as simple posterboard costumes and masks and no-sew fabric costumes. In addition, this section includes suggestions for using the children's own clothes, thus minimizing the need for making costumes. The body of the script text includes suggestions for props as needed. Often props can be pantomimed; a few are mandatory. Use discretion based upon prop availability as to what the audience needs to understand the play. Teachers can make many props from posterboard or cardboard and markers.

This section also provides ideas for songs, poems, sketches, and play-themed presentations that teachers can use in conjunction with a play performance. When this section recommends factual or poetic presentation ideas, it also provides suggestions for reference and resource books when subjects cannot be readily researched in encyclopedias. Sometimes the performance ideas included here utilize materials from activities suggested in the "Write It" or "Explore It" sections of the Teacher's Notes.

Finally, this section gives teachers and play leaders ideas for ways to prepare students for play performance so that children can get the most out of both the content of the play and the performing experience. It gives suggestions for background information to help students understand and fully enjoy the play's content. When these ideas are coupled with the cross-curricular ideas for exploring the play's theme and content contained in the "Write It," "Explore It," and "Read About It" sections of the supplementary material, play performance becomes an interdisciplinary exercise that aids in children's intellectual and cultural development while building confidence, self-esteem, and teamwork.

WRITE IT

The writing activities keep in mind the developing writing skills of students, as well as the differing skill levels that exist in any class regardless of grade level. Teachers can adapt some activities for use with any number of plays. These include riddles, haiku, couplets, acrostics, similes, alliteration poems, and poems about the senses. The writing activities focus on developing skills such as noun identification, letter sounds, adjectives and other parts of speech, as well as reinforcing basic sentence structure.

EXPLORE IT

This section provides one or more cross-curricular activities to enable students to further explore the play's subject matter. Math, art, music, and cooking activities are among the offerings included here.

READ ABOUT IT

This section gives a teacher or play director literature resources to use in conjunction with both preparation and exploration of the play's subject matter. Resources can be fiction or nonfiction, depending upon the play's subject matter.

See the end of the book for help in creating publicity pieces. Two templates located at the end of the book can help you to create your own play invitations, posters, and programs.

IX

Warm-up: *Developing Speaking Skills*

Here are some warm-up activities to prepare students for performance of any play by helping develop students' poise, speaking ability, and confidence:

1. **Oral Book Reviews**—Assign children book report or review opportunities at least once a month. These oral presentations do not need to be limited to the standard restatement of plot and whether the child liked or disliked the book, but can be creative. For instance, ask children to create a puppet for a character in the book that they can then use as part of the oral review.

   Alternatively, the child could create a diorama scene from the book and then incorporate the diorama and description of it into the book report.

2. **Demonstrations**—Ask children to demonstrate how to do something. These can be called "how-to" talks. The child can demonstrate just about anything from how to make a snack to how to address an envelope. These presentations need be only a few minutes long but they provide not only speaking opportunities, but the learning experience of analyzing an activity, discerning the steps involved, and organizing presentation of the material.

3. **Science Speak**—Oral presentation of science experiments is a subject-specific version of the demonstration activity described above. Children do an experiment at home and then show the class how to do the experiment so that audience members can try it at home as well.

4. **Poetry Recitation**—One of the best ways to build speaking ability is by assigning weekly poetry memorization and recitation. Choose poems (or parts of poems) no longer than four lines long for children to learn each week. They receive the poem on Monday and must recite it for the class on Friday.

   Encourage eye contact and volume. Over the course of several months, even the shyest children experience considerable growth in speaking ability and confidence.

5. **Lit Skits**—Ask children to work in groups to create a scene with dialogue from the literature book they are reading as a class or in reading groups. This process helps children begin thinking about how dialogue and pantomime help tell a story, as well as what kinds of props and scenery are necessary to help an audience understand what is happening on stage. Students can also create skits as an extension of history-based social studies classwork. Children tell a story from the history lessons they are studying by turning them into a skit.

6. **Advertise It**—Ask children to work in groups to create an oral (either television or radio) advertisement for a book they are reading or about a health or nutrition lesson in which they are involved.

X

7. **Make the News**—Have children take a real news event from the newspaper or school community, or an event from the historical social studies curriculum, to create a newscast about the event.

8. **News Story Time**—Every other week, have children read the local paper to find a short news or lifestyle story that they will read at home with their parents. The child cuts out the story, brings it to school, and describes the story orally to the class, recounting at least three things he or she learned from the story.

Some combination of the above oral activities, used on an ongoing basis, serve to improve the children's oral communication skills and their speaking poise and confidence, as well as reinforcing curriculum studies.

Hints on Play Preparation

When you are ready to begin preparing children to perform a particular play, the following method works well.

1. **Tell the children the story line of the play.** Then, read it to them if they are too young to read it themselves. If their reading skills permit, copy the script for each child, randomly assign parts (for read-through purposes only), and have the children read the play aloud.

   As you do this, in some plays you will come across places in which script dialogue needs to be written by the students. Explain to them what kinds of things the actors for these sections will need to say or explain. (The script text itself will tell you what needs to be included.) See if students want to volunteer to work on those lines. As an alternative, you can do the writing as a class before the second read-through.

   Explain commonly used play terms such as the following to children and show them examples of each.

   ad-lib—making up lines as the actor goes

   pantomime—using gestures instead of words to express something

   mimic—imitating or copying someone or something

2. **Assign each student a part.** Consider each child's effectiveness when doing the read-through as you assign longer or more challenging parts. Another consideration is available costuming. If the costuming for a play requires different-colored clothing, you might want to give parts to children who have clothing in the available colors.

   Note the student part assignments on your copy of the script. If your students are non-readers, give each child a copy of his or her part(s). Ask them to work on the parts overnight with a parent's or other adult's help before doing another read-through. Some script lines include words challenging to young children; however, exposure to these words in context is essential for vocabulary development. Simple definitions appear in the margin near those words for your convenience in explaining those words. This not only helps the child understand the lines but is also a teaching tool.

If some lines are awkward for children, encourage them to discuss the lines with a parent or with you to develop line changes so the words are easier to say. Any change that works for the child also works for the play, as long as the meaning is generally the same. Sometimes you will need to cut part of a line or sentence to make it easier. Feel free to do this as needed.

3. **Hold a read-through of the play with students reading or reciting their assigned parts.** Then move to your staging area and place children in the proper positions for the opening of the play. Go through the entire play with children stating their lines as you stage it.

At this point, also discuss with children what props, if any, their characters need and ask for volunteers to make those props at home or in free time in class. Also have children start thinking about what resources for costumes and accessories they have at home. You will be surprised at what they can bring in.

4. **Now that the play is staged, the next rehearsal is a run-through.** Use the run-through to emphasize entrances and exits (correcting any problems that become apparent) and volume and clarity of spoken lines. By this rehearsal only children with multiple lines should be allowed to use a script.

5. **Use the next rehearsals to polish the play.** Emphasize slow, loud statement of lines. Remind children to face the audience even if they are supposed to be speaking to another actor on stage. Remind them to be aware of the line or play activity that precedes their lines. You will know when the play is ready to perform. Children will peak and be ready after two to three polishing rehearsals.

As you ready children for performance, remember that the play is a tool. You need not be too rigid in using the script. View it as a resource that is adaptable to meet your needs. If you need fewer speaking lines, cut some out or have actors double up on lines. If a line seems too long or difficult, have the child think about ways to make it shorter and easier to say. If you need more lines, divide some up or, better yet, ask the children to see if they can think of places where a line can be added. They almost always can. Once children get involved in the play process, the play becomes theirs. The more they make it their own, the more they get from the play production experience.

CELEBRATING THE SEASONS

THE PUZZLED PUMPKINS

PLAYERS

PUMPKINS 1–29

LITTLE PUMPKIN

Teacher's Notes Begin on Page 6

SCRIPT

As the play opens, PUMPKINS *are located about the stage, preferably arranged on steps or risers to approximate the look of a pumpkin patch. Actors will not need to move from place to place, so they should be placed so each is visible to the audience.*

PUMPKIN 1 *(waving arms and wailing dramatically):* Oh, woe is me!

PUMPKIN 2 *(hands sweeping to show rest of patch):* Woe is you? Woe is us.

PUMPKIN 3: Here we are stuck in the patch, just growing and growing.

PUMPKIN 4 *(complaining):* And for what? We sit here like a bunch of old orange bumps on a log waiting for someone to come along and pick us out of the crowd.

PUMPKIN 5 *(disgustedly):* And won't that be fun! We spend our childhoods sitting here watching life pass us by.

PUMPKIN 6: Then they cut us free to fulfill our grown-up purpose.

PUMPKIN 7: Yes, we grow up so that they can poke at us, yank out our seeds, boil us, or bake us. What a life!

LITTLE PUMPKIN *(bewildered):* But who are "they"?

PUMPKIN 8: "They" are people. You know, humans. They take us from the vine and . . . *(snapping fingers)* just like that, it's over. *(Dramatically)* Oh, woe is us!

PUMPKIN 9: You know, I think you guys are looking at this thing all wrong. We pumpkins are part of a grand and glorious tradition.

TRADITION: way of doing things

3

NATIVE: naturally found in a place

PILGRIM: English people who came to North America in 1620

JACK-O'-LANTERN: lighted, hollow pumpkin with a cut-out face

DRAMATIC: in a strong way

CENTERPIECE: table decoration

NUTMEG: a spicy seed used to flavor food

JOB OPPORTUNITIES: chances for future jobs or work

LITTLE PUMPKIN: We are? What tradition? Tell me.

PUMPKIN 10: Well, we are a native American fruit. We were here when the Pilgrims arrived.

PUMPKIN 11: And we play an important part in more than one fun holiday tradition.

PUMPKIN 12: Yes, I've always wanted to grow up to be a jack-o'-lantern with a happy face.

PUMPKIN 13: Personally, I'd prefer to be part of a dramatic centerpiece on a Thanksgiving dinner table.

PUMPKIN 14: Well, not me. I was born to be a mouth-watering pumpkin bread.

PUMPKIN 1 *(negatively):* What kind of life is that? Three gulps and you are gone.

PUMPKIN 15: No, no, no. You are still not seeing the point. We pumpkins have a lot to offer.

PUMPKIN 16: Yes, we are many things to many people. Me? I like to think of myself as a trim, healthful side dish.

PUMPKIN 17: That's true. What could be better than a slab of baked pumpkin with just a sprinkle of brown sugar and nutmeg?

PUMPKIN 18 *(spreading hands to give credit to previous speakers):* And, besides all these fabulous job opportunities, think of how important we are in stories.

PUMPKIN 19: Yes, without us, where would Cinderella be?

PUMPKIN 20: I'll tell you where. Without us, she'd never get out of the garden.

PUMPKIN 21: And don't forget about Mother Goose. Where would she be without us?

4

PUMPKIN 22: That's true. Remember "Peter, Peter, pumpkin-eater . . . "?

PUMPKIN 23 *(thinking carefully):* Fellow pumpkins, maybe some of us haven't been looking at this whole situation the right way.

PUMPKIN 24: Yes, when you get right down to it, right down through history we've been playing a fine part.

HISTORY: study of the past

PUMPKIN 25: I guess that's true. There are a lot worse things than sitting on a dinner table no matter what part of the meal you are.

PUMPKIN 26: Well, I hope I get to choose the job in my future.

PUMPKIN 27: Why is that?

PUMPKIN 28: Because if I had my choice, I'd like to be a nice slab of steaming pumpkin pie.

PUMPKIN 29: Yeah, à la mode—you know, with ice cream on top.

PUMPKIN 27: With such a wide range of job opportunities, how will we choose?

LITTLE PUMPKIN: Well, I don't care which job I get. I always say, "get a job and do it well." That's the best way.

ALL PUMPKINS: That's the pumpkin way!

The End

TEACHER'S NOTES

PERFORM IT

You can costume your pumpkins easily by making large orange posterboard pumpkins that hang on the children's chests. Each child draws in his or her own face with markers. You can have Pumpkins 1–8 make sad or crabby-looking faces on one side of the posterboard. At the play's end, they can turn them over to expose smiling, happy faces like the rest of the patch. Alternatively, you can use orange no-sew tunics cut round at the bottom and, again, use marker to create the faces.

An enjoyable way to extend this play performance is to open and/or close the play with small group recitation or reading of several poems from Jack Prelutsky's holiday collections, such as *It's Halloween* or *It's Thanksgiving.* Choose those poems appropriate to your seasonal use of this play.

This play can be used in conjunction with any fall activities or events. It is suitable for Halloween and Thanksgiving performances as well as other harvest festival celebrations. To help prepare children for the play, talk with them about this special native American gourd. Not only was it here when the Pilgrims arrived, the pumpkin has become a part of Halloween,

Thanksgiving, and Christmas traditions. Have them think about how pumpkin is used by people during the fall and winter months. Finally, ask them to think about stories they know in which pumpkins play a part. Besides *Cinderella,* and *Mother Goose,* and *Charlie Brown's Great Pumpkin,* there is a myriad of stories in which pumpkins play an important role.

WRITE IT

Have each child draw his or her own pumpkin person. As a writing exercise, ask children to write a short story or paragraph describing their own pumpkin persons—how they feel, what they are doing, what their "career" plans are. Students might get ideas for their stories from the text of the play.

EXPLORE IT

Pumpkin season provides fun opportunities for exploring math creatively. Ask children to bring in enough pumpkins so that you have at least one pumpkin for every two children. You will also need string for this activity. Have children measure and weigh pumpkins, count pumpkin seeds, and make class graphs of the results. Examples of the questions they can answer are:

- *How tall is the pumpkin?*
- *How big around (circumference) is the pumpkin?*
- *How wide (diameter) is the pumpkin?*
- *How much does the pumpkin weigh?*
- *How many seeds does the pumpkin hold?*

Once you do your "practical" math with the pumpkin you might want to continue the exercise with some cooking math by making pumpkin bread.

Pumpkin Bread

$1/2$	cup vegetable oil
$1\,1/2$	cups sugar
2	eggs
1	teaspoon vanilla
1	cup pumpkin
2	cups flour
$1/2$	teaspoon salt
1	teaspoon baking soda
$1/2$	teaspoon cinnamon
$1/2$	teaspoon ginger
$1/4$	teaspoon cloves
$1/4$	teaspoon nutmeg

Cream oil and sugar. Add eggs and vanilla and mix well. Add pumpkin and mix well. Add dry ingredients and stir until well mixed. Grease and flour a loaf pan, pour in batter, and bake at 350°F for 60 to 75 minutes or until toothpick comes out clean.

READ ABOUT IT

Johnston, Tony. *The Vanishing Pumpkin.*
G. P. Putnam's Sons, 1983.

Miller, Edna. *Mousekin's Golden House.*
Simon & Schuster, 1964.

Ray, Mary Lyn. *Pumpkins.* Harcourt
Brace Jovanovich, 1992.

Titherington, Jeanne. *Pumpkin
Pumpkin.* Greenwillow Books, 1986.

PUMPKIN WEIGH-IN™

7

BRINGING IN THE HARVEST

PLAYERS

STRANGERS 1–6   PEA FARMERS 1–2

POTATO FARMERS 1–6   GREEN BEAN FARMERS 1–2

CARROT FARMERS 1–6   CORN FARMERS 1–2

ONION FARMERS 1–6

Teacher's Notes
Begin on
Page 14

SCRIPT

POTATO FARMERS *are looking over their crop, holding potatoes and shaking heads.* STRANGERS *enter as* FARMERS *shake their heads.*

STRANGER 1: Good day, Farmers.

POTATO FARMER 1 *(sad):* What's so good about it?

POTATO FARMER 2 *(discouraged):* Yes, look at this crop. This is terrible.

STRANGER 2: What's wrong with it?

POTATO FARMER 3: What's wrong with it? We only got potatoes. That's what's wrong with it.

POTATO FARMER 4: You see, we planted peas, carrots, onions, *and* potatoes.

POTATO FARMER 5: We could have had a feast, but all we got were lumpy, brown potatoes.

STRANGER 3: We like potatoes. Can we have one?

POTATO FARMER 6: One? Take as many as you like. We'll be eating potatoes for months.
(STRANGERS *take one potato.*)

STRANGER 4: Thank you so much for the potato. You are very generous.
(POTATO FARMERS *exit and* CARROT FARMERS *enter carrying carrots.*)

STRANGER 1: Good day, Farmers.

CARROT FARMER 1: What's so good about it?

CROP: plants grown for use

9

CARROT FARMER 2: Yes, look at this crop. This is terrible.

STRANGER 2: What's wrong with it?

CARROT FARMER 3: What's wrong with it? We only got carrots. That's what's wrong with it.

CARROT FARMER 4: We planted eggplant, corn, potatoes, onions, *and* carrots.

FEAST: a large, very grand meal

CARROT FARMER 5: We could have had a feast, but all we got were these skinny, little carrots.

STRANGER 3: We like carrots. Can we have one or two?

CARROT FARMER 6: Take as many as you like. We'll be eating carrots for months.

GENEROUS: kind and unselfish

STRANGER 4: Thank you for the carrots. You are very generous.
(CARROT FARMERS *exit while* ONION FARMERS *enter carrying onions.*)

STRANGER 1: Good day, Farmers.

ONION FARMER 1: What's so good about it?

ONION FARMER 2: Yes, look at this crop. This is terrible.

STRANGER 2: What's wrong with it?

ONION FARMER 3: What's wrong with it? We only got onions. That's what's wrong with it.

ONION FARMER 4: We planted potatoes, carrots, green beans, corn, *and* onions.

ONION FARMER 5: We could have had a feast, but all we got were these stinky onions.

STRANGER 3: We like onions. Can we have one?

ONION FARMER 6: Take as many as you like. We've got enough to last for months.

STRANGER 4: Thank you so much for the onion. You are very generous.
(ONION FARMERS *exit while* PEA FARMERS, GREEN BEAN FARMERS, *and* CORN FARMERS *enter, each carrying a sample of his or her crop.*)

STRANGER 1: Good day, Farmers.

PEA FARMER 1: What's so good about it? I just harvested my crop, and all I got were peas. I hate peas.

STRANGER 5: I like peas. I'll take a pod or two.

PEA FARMER 2: Be my guest. Have some pea pods.
(PEA FARMER *hands over a few pods.*)

GREEN BEAN FARMER 1: I just harvested my crop, and all I got were green beans. My family will not eat green beans, so what good is it?

STRANGER 5: I like green beans. I'll take a few.

GREEN BEAN FARMER 2: Be my guest. Have a few green beans.
(GREEN BEAN FARMER *hands over a few beans.*)

CORN FARMER 1: I just harvested my crop, and all I got was corn. I am very tired of eating corn.

STRANGER 5: I like corn. I'll take an ear.

CORN FARMER 2: Be my guest. Have an ear.
(*Enter* POTATO, CARROT, *and* ONION FARMERS.)

STRANGER 1 (*pointing in the direction of entering* POTATO, CARROT, *and* ONION FARMERS): Look! Here come the other farmers.
(*Other* FARMERS *enter carrying their crops, shaking their heads, and looking disgusted.*)

STRANGER 6: You farmers don't see what you have here. What you have here is a feast!

POD: part of plant that holds seeds

STRANGER 2: Get us a pot and some water and we'll show you.
(*Two* FARMERS *give* STRANGERS *a large pot, spoon, and water pitcher, and pretend to pour water into the pot.*)

STRANGER 4: Now we need a little fire.
(*Two other* FARMERS *pantomime the starting of a fire under the pot.*)

STRANGER 6: And now for some of our vegetable magic.

STRANGER 1: In goes the dependable potato, the soup pot's best friend.

STRANGER 2: In goes the tasty, sweet carrot, that healthiest of roots.

STRANGER 3: In goes the aromatic onion, the jewel of any chef's kitchen.

STRANGER 4: And for flavor, nutrition, and fiber, in go the peas, green beans, and corn.

STRANGER 5: Smell that stew. Mmmm, mmmmm. Now this will make an excellent meal.

POTATO FARMER 1: My, but that stew does smell good.

CARROT FARMER 1: I am soooo hungry.

ONION FARMER 1: Oh, I can tell that my onion made all the difference in that wonderful stew.
(STRANGERS *pantomime serving the stew and* FARMERS *pantomime eating, shaking heads "yes," and ad-libbing phrases such as "so delicious," "Can I have more?" and "mmmmmm good."*)

DEPENDABLE: always the same

AROMATIC: strong smelling

NUTRITION: growth and energy from good foods

FIBER: helps remove wastes from body

12

PEA FARMER 2: Perhaps if we all share our crops, we could make such a grand soup to share.

GREEN BEAN FARMER 2 (*to* POTATO *and* ONION FARMERS)*:* We certainly have enough green beans, and I'll bet you have enough potatoes and onions.

CORN FARMER 2 (*to* CARROT FARMERS)*:* And I'll throw in some corn if you'll throw in some carrots.

POTATO FARMER 2: Oh, what a feast we will have!

STRANGER 3: You may use this pot, if you please. And thank you for the vegetables that made such fine soup.
(*One* FARMER *from each group delivers vegetables to the pot.*)

CARROT FARMER 3: I think we learned something today about what makes a good harvest.

ONION FARMER 3: Yes, so long as we have good neighbors to share with, there is never a bad crop.

The End

TEACHER'S NOTES

PERFORM IT

Costuming this play is simple. Have Farmers wear jeans or skirts, depending upon gender and preference, and plaid shirts as available. Straw hats look good. The Strangers can wear simple clothing (plain-colored tan or black pants or skirts and white shirts) and aprons, since they become the cooks.

To expand the performance of this play, consider one or more of these ideas:

- Have children write "Who am I?" vegetable riddles to tell the audience. Encourage audience participation by having them guess the vegetable described.

- Have a group of three children perform a pantomimed story—telling how a seed grows. All three mimes start in a ball-like position on the floor. This is a three-part pantomime that can be done to simple text, such as: "First you plant a seed. *(First child scrunches on floor in a ball.)* You water the seed and the root and stem begin to grow. (Second child starts to stand up straight, arms at side.)* Then the leaves begin to grow." *(Third child "grows" to standing position and puts out arms like leaves.)*

- Using a Big Book version of *Growing Vegetable Soup,* have children read the story to the audience while other children hold up poster-sized food props as a food is mentioned.

This play can be used any time of year in conjunction with reading literature such as *Stone Soup* or *Growing Vegetable Soup.* It is also suitable for Thanksgiving celebrations and any harvest-themed or other food-themed events, such as nutrition studies.

WRITE IT

Several writing activities are appropriate with this play. You may consider a riddle writing activity using vegetables as your subject matter. If you do this, have each child bring in a vegetable to examine closely as he or she writes the riddle.

Example:

Q. I am long and shiny and purple.
I have little leaves at one end.
Inside I am seedy and tan-colored.
What am I?

A. An eggplant

A slightly more time-consuming writing task is for children to write fold-out book stories of how a seed grows. (One of these stories could be used as the text for

14

the pantomime play expander described in "Perform It.")

EXPLORE IT

The perfect class activity for this play is to have children make vegetable or "stone" soup. Children always enjoy this and it offers an excellent opportunity to talk about nutritious foods. An easy way to do this is to have children bring in fresh vegetables of their choice (e.g., zucchini, peas, green beans, green onions, celery, carrots, and potatoes). Children shuck peas and chop other vegetables into one-inch pieces using plastic knives. One child brings in a can of corn and another several bouillon cubes. Bring three to four inches of water to a boil with vegetables and bouillon cubes and let simmer for about thirty minutes. Season with two teaspoons garlic powder and salt and pepper to taste.

Alternatively, use this play as a starting point for discussing nutritious foods and healthy snacks. Have children bring in bananas, apples, and other fruits and vegetables; peanut butter; and bread, and show them how to make peanut butter and banana sandwiches (a big hit), peanut butter–smeared apple slices, peanut butter–filled celery strips, and the like. Be sure to check whether children have any allergies to these foods before serving them in class.

READ ABOUT IT

Brown, Marcia. *Stone Soup*. Macmillan, 1947.

Ehlert, Lois. *Growing Vegetable Soup*. Harcourt Brace Jovanovich, 1987.

Parkinson, Kathy. *The Turnip: A Russian Folktale*. Albert Whitman, 1986.

VIVALDI AND THE SOUND OF SPRING

VIVALDI AND THE SOUND OF SPRING

PLAYERS

TEACHERS 1–3

MAESTRO ANTONIO VIVALDI

STRINGS 1–6

VISITORS 1–20

Teacher's Notes Begin on Page 22

SCRIPT

As the play begins, the girls' orchestra is seated. Each holds a cardboard string instrument prop. Place several music stands among the girls, if available. They can be pantomiming practice of a Vivaldi piece, if you choose. Tape the piece and use a cassette recorder that you or a stage assistant can press on and off easily. For this play, you will also need to have readily available for similar playing the first thirty to sixty seconds of each of the first movements of Vivaldi's Four Seasons *concertos.*

(*Enter* TEACHERS 1–3.)

TEACHER 1 (*clapping hands*): Girls, girls. Today is our big open house. You will have visitors all day.

TEACHER 2: Please be as helpful as you can to Maestro Vivaldi. He is trying to finish some music for tomorrow's big concert.

TEACHER 3: Here comes the first group of visitors now. They are here to see our school and especially our famous all-girl, string orchestra led by our famous teacher, Maestro Antonio Vivaldi. (*Enter* VISITORS 1–5 *and exit* TEACHERS 1–3. *At the same time but from another part of the stage,* VIVALDI *enters with some white papers that are supposed to be new compositions.*)

VIVALDI (*passing papers to orchestra*): Girls, visitors. Perhaps you can help me. I am working on several compositions.

OPEN HOUSE: event for visitors to come to school

MAESTRO: a person skilled in an art—here a writer of music

CONCERT: musical performance

ORCHESTRA: a special musical performance group

COMPOSITIONS: long pieces of written music

CONCERTO: a piece of music played by a solo instrument and an orchestra

ORPHANAGE: home for children who do not have parents

THREATENING: warning of trouble or harm

PIECE: a written work of music

STRING 1: Are these the four concertos you call the *Four Seasons?*

VIVALDI: Yes, they are, but I am having trouble figuring out which season is which. And I think spring is the most difficult for me to write.

STRING 1: Let's play the music and see what we all think.
(VIVALDI *nods.* STRINGS *raise cardboard versions of instruments and pretend to play as the sounds of the winter concerto are played.* VIVALDI *conducts by waving his hands to the music. When the music stops, he waves hands as though he has told the girls to stop playing. They put their instruments in their laps.)*

VISITOR 1: That was beautiful, girls! You all play so well.

VISITOR 2: Well, you know, this orphanage is famous for its excellent all-girl orchestra.

VIVALDI: But let's get back to the point. What do you think? What season was that?

VISITOR 3: That is a very hard question, Maestro. I hear many things in the music.

VISITOR 4: I heard sounds that seemed dark and threatening.

VISITOR 5: Parts of the music sound like a great storm coming.

STRING 2: That's it! I think our visitors have very good ears. I think that was winter, Maestro, with its dark, threatening storms.

VIVALDI: Very good. That's settled. Now, girls, the next piece.
(*He raises his hands to conduct while girls raise their instruments.* VISITORS 1–5 *leave as* VISITORS 6–10 *enter. The taped music is played; it is the first part of the first movement of the autumn concerto. When the music stops,* VIVALDI *waves his hands to stop, and the girls put their instruments in their laps.)*

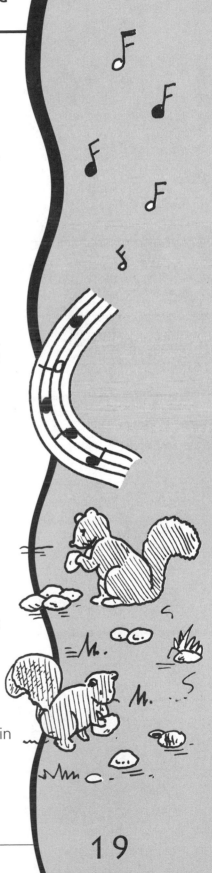

VISITOR 6: That was beautiful, girls! You all play so well.

VISITOR 7: Well, you know, this orphanage is famous for its excellent all-girl orchestra.

VIVALDI: But let's get back to the point. What do you think? What season was that?

VISITOR 8: That's a very hard question, Maestro. I hear many things in the music.

VISITOR 9: The music seems very active and busy.

VISITOR 10: Part of the music sounds as though creatures are busy making ready for a coming change.

STRING 3: That's it! I think our visitors have very good ears. I think that was autumn, Maestro, with the sounds of squirrels busily preparing for winter.

VIVALDI: Very good. That's settled. Now, girls, the next piece.
(*He raises his hands to conduct while the girls raise their instruments.* VISITORS 6–10 *leave as* VISITORS 11–15 *enter. The taped music begins at the first part of the first concerto for summer. When the music ends, the girls put down their instruments.*)

VISITOR 11: That was beautiful, girls! You all play so well.

VISITOR 12: Well, you know, this orphanage is famous for its excellent all-girl orchestra.

VIVALDI: But let's get back to the point. What do you think? What season was that?

VISITOR 13: That is a very hard question, Maestro. I hear many things in the music.

VISITOR 14: I heard sounds that seemed lazy and tired.

19

VISITOR 15: Parts of the music sounded like the sleepiness you feel when it's hot.

STRING 4: That's it! I think our visitors have very good ears. I think that was summer, Maestro, with its slow, hot breezes.
(*Exit* VISITORS 11–15 *and enter* VISITORS 16–20.)

VIVALDI: Very good, but now comes the most difficult of all. All that is left is spring.

STRING 5: But spring is a wonderful time of year, Maestro.

STRING 6: Yes, it's a time of busy, happy activity in the bright, warm sunshine.

POSSIBILITIES: things that one might be able to do

STRING 1: Spring is so full of possibilities!

VISITORS 16–20: [*Each* VISITOR *makes one statement about what spring is like. These statements should be different from those made by* STRINGS 5–6. *The entire class can work on these lines or the individual players can make up their own lines. Examples are:*

- *In spring, the trees and flowers are budding.*

- *In spring, the animals are having babies.*]

(*While these exchanges are underway,* VIVALDI *is busy making notes and checking the girls' music on their stands.*)

VIVALDI: These are all very good ideas. Let's hope that you hear spring in this next piece. [*Optional:* If not, it's back to the composition book for me.]
(*Girls raise instruments and* VIVALDI *raises arms to conduct. The* VISITORS *look on. The taped music plays the first part of the first movement of the spring concerto. When the music ends, the girls put their instruments in their laps.*)

STRING 1: Oh, Maestro, that's it! That's definitely spring.

VISITORS AND STRINGS *(all together ad-libbing words of congratulations and stating simple things about how the music sounds like spring):* It's wonderful. So playful. So full of life. It is definitely spring.
(TEACHERS 1–3 *rush in.*)

TEACHER 1: Maestro, we heard your music from the hall.

TEACHER 2: It is wonderful—more wonderful than any before.

TEACHER 3: I was sure that I heard the sounds of spring in that last piece.

TEACHER 1: Yes. The music reminded me of trees as they bud with new green leaves.

TEACHER 2: It reminded me of wildflowers blooming.

TEACHER 3: Oh, it made me happy just to hear it. Can you play it again? Can you play the sounds of spring?

VIVALDI *(smiling and proud):* With pleasure. Girls?
[*He raises his hands to conduct, and the girls raise their instruments to play. Taped music of the first movement of the spring concerto is played again as one student states over the sounds of the music:* Thank you for coming to our play. May it bring a little spring to your day.]

The End

TEACHER'S NOTES

PERFORM IT

To costume this play, have Strings wear black pants or skirts and white blouses. Vivaldi can have a red wig and the same black and white attire. The Teachers and Visitors can dress in any clothing with an effort to make it look old-fashioned, with long skirts for girls and dark slacks and white shirts for boys. Vests are a nice costume addition.

Expand this performance with composer and music facts. A student might hold up a picture of Vivaldi while other students take turns stating different facts of the composer's life, such as:

- Antonio Vivaldi was born in Venice, Italy, in 1678.
- He played the violin and wrote musical pieces.
- When in Venice, he was teacher and conductor for a famous all-girls' orchestra at the Pietà orphanage.
- He was known as the Red Priest because he had fiery red hair and he was an ordained priest.
- One of his most famous series of compositions is the *Four Seasons* concerto series upon which this play is based.
- He died in 1741 in Vienna, Austria, at the age of sixty-three.

Other students might explain the nature of the concerto musical form upon which this play is based. Informational statements might include:

- A concerto is a musical composition for an orchestra.
- An orchestra today has strings, brass, woodwinds, and percussion.
- A concerto features a solo instrument against the orchestra.
- Concertos can feature any instrument, but violin and piano concertos are common.
- The concertos in *Four Seasons* are for the violin.
- A concerto has three different parts called movements.

To prepare children to perform this play, you will want to introduce not only the composer Vivaldi (see facts above), but also what an orchestra is and the four sections of instruments that make up an orchestra (strings, woodwinds, brass, and percussion). The *Four Seasons* music itself is known as program music. That means it was written to evoke a particular feeling, place, or time. The text of the play explores this concept by helping children see how the music reflects the way the different seasons actually sound and how things that occur in them, such as blooming flowers, might sound if you could hear them. Use the "Explore It" activity as a way to have children become more familiar with the music itself.

WRITE IT

A season-themed writing activity is to have children write a traditional Japanese haiku. A haiku is a three-lined poem with five syllables in the first line, seven syllables in the second line, and five syllables in the third line. In traditional haiku, the subject is nature and at least one word in the poem is a "season" word—that is, for winter, the word might be *winter* or a word reminding one of winter such as *snow*.

Example:

The chill winds blow by
Whipping up the dead leaves and
Bringing winter's snow.

Another writing activity is to have children write a simple biography report on Vivaldi's life. The simple form that works best with young children is the five-sentence report. It includes an opening sentence describing the report subject, three sentences with fact information, and a final summary sentence. With younger students, you can write the report as a class activity on the board, and they can copy it. Have them draw a picture of Vivaldi to accompany the report.

Example:

Vivaldi was a famous composer.
He was born in 1678.
He played the violin.

He taught a girls' orchestra.
This is how Vivaldi was important to music.

EXPLORE IT

As children prepare for this play, an art activity that provides both introduction to the *Four Seasons* music and allows for creativity is explorative and fun. Try having children paint a series of "season" watercolors while listening to the different Vivaldi *Four Season* concertos. First, have them listen only to the first movement of one of the season pieces. Then, have them create an abstract artwork while listening to the same music. What they hear in the music, they paint. Have them move their paintbrushes across the paper in time with the music. You might do this "watercolor by the music" for each season or just for the season of your choice, as class time permits.

READ ABOUT IT

Hayes, Ann. *Meet the Orchestra.* Voyager Books, 1991.

Krull, Kathleen. *Lives of the Musicians: Good Times, Bad Times (And What the Neighbors Thought).* Harcourt Brace & Company, 1993. (Section on Vivaldi for reading aloud)

Kuskin, Karla. *The Philharmonic Gets Dressed.* HarperTrophy, 1982.

23

IT ALL STARTS WITH THE SUN

PLAYERS

CHILDREN **1–9**
SUN
SUNSPOTS **1–3**
PLANTS **1–4**
COWS **1–4**

FOSSIL FUELS **1–5**
MOON
SUNRISE
SUNSET
EARTH

Teacher's Notes Begin on Page 30

SCRIPT

As the play opens, CHILDREN 1–9 *are seated randomly about the stage.* SUN *and* SUNSPOTS 1–3 *are located at center stage.*

CHILD 1: Boy, is it hot! I'm sweating like crazy.

CHILD 2: I think this is what they call a "heat wave."

CHILD 3: Well, I'd like to wave good-bye to this heat.

CHILD 4: It's so hot I don't feel like doing anything.

CHILD 5: Yeah, we've been waiting for the warm weather, and now it's too hot to skate or bike.

CHILD 6: I wish that old sun would just go on vacation for a day.

CHILD 7: Then it would cool off, and we could have some fun.

ALL CHILDREN: What a summer bummer!

SUN: Hey!

CHILD 1: Did you hear something?

SUN: Hey, you kids down there!

CHILD 2: I heard something too. Who is it?
(CHILDREN *all look around puzzled.*)

SUN: It's me.

CHILD 3: Me, who?

SUNSPOTS: dark spots on the sun's surface

FOSSIL FUEL: a material from inside the Earth used to make heat or power

HEAT WAVE: more than one day of very hot weather

SUN: Me, the sun.

CHILDREN *(all together):* The sun!

CHILD 7: Don't be silly. The sun is 93 million miles away. You can feel its heat and see its light, but it doesn't talk.

CHILD 5: How do you know? Maybe it's some kind of miracle.

CHILD 8: The sun is a whole bunch of hot hydrogen gas—and hydrogen gas just doesn't talk.

CHILD 9: I don't know. Some grown-ups say that people who talk a lot are full of hot air. That sounds a lot like what you're talking about.

SUN: I don't know how it happened, but I am the sun and I am talking to you.

CHILDREN *(all together):* Wow!

CHILD 9: What do you want to talk about?

SUNSPOT 1: Well, you do nothing but complain about the sun.

SUNSPOT 2: We're sorry you are hot, but we don't think you appreciate what you have because of the sun.

SUNSPOT 3: And most of what the sun gives you is good.

CHILD 1: Tell us about it.

SUN: Why don't we have a few of our friends tell you about all we do?

CHILDREN *(ad-libbing and talking together):* Okay. We're ready. We're listening.

SUNSPOT 1: Let the parade begin.

CHILD 2: Look, here come some plants.

Enter PLANTS 1–4.

PLANT 1: The sun told us you all needed some straightening out.

MIRACLE: a wonderful happening that is impossible to explain

HYDROGEN: gas that burns easily

APPRECIATE: to be thankful for

PLANT 2: We don't want the sun to go away, not even for a day.

PLANT 3: Without the sun, the Earth would freeze and seeds would not sprout.

PLANT 4: Without the sun, we couldn't grow the fruits and vegetables that you eat.

CHILD 5: Oh, that's okay. We'll just eat milk and eggs and meat.

PLANT 1: You think so? Well, here come some friends who can set you straight about that.
(*Exit* PLANTS 1-4 *and enter* COWS 1–4.)

COW 1: You children don't understand. If the sun were not here to make plants grow, we wouldn't be here to give you milk and food to eat.

COW 2: Yes. Without the sun to make grass and plants grow, we would have nothing to eat.

COW 3: And if we have nothing to eat, we can't live. And if we can't live, we can't make milk for you to drink.

COW 4: And besides, without the sun, we'd all freeze no matter how many layers of fur we had.

CHILD 5: We wouldn't freeze. We'd just turn on the heat.
(COWS *laugh.*)

COW 2: Maybe you want to think about that again. I see some friends coming who can clue you in on that.
(*Exit* COWS *and enter* FOSSIL FUELS 1–5.)

FOSSIL FUEL 1: We hear you kids think you can get by without the sun just by turning on the heat.

FOSSIL FUEL 2: Don't you realize you get your heat from the sun, no matter how you turn it on?

CLUE: something that helps you find an answer

27

FOSSIL FUEL 3: Yes, if you use solar power, that is power collected from the sun's rays.

FOSSIL FUEL 4: And if you burn coal or wood for a fire, your heat comes from either a tree that the sun grew or a fossil deep in the Earth.

FOSSIL FUEL 5: And fossils deep in the Earth used to be living things that grew because of the sun. So you see, it all starts with the sun.

FOSSIL FUEL 1: Well, we've got to go now, but here are some friends to tell you about other things the sun gives you.
(*Exit* FOSSIL FUELS *and enter* MOON, SUNRISE, SUNSET, *and* EARTH.)

MOON: If you kids sent the sun on vacation, you would never see me.

CHILDREN (*ad-libbing, speaking at the same time*): Why? I/We don't understand. How does that work?

MOON: When you see me, you are seeing the sun's light reflecting off me.

SUNRISE: And what about me? What would life be like if you could never see a beautiful sunrise?

SUNSET: Don't forget me. A sunset is at least as pretty as a sunrise.

COAL: a black mineral burnt for fuel

FOSSIL: hardened plant or animal part from long ago

EARTH: But down to basics, kids. Without the sun, there wouldn't be life as we know it. The Earth wouldn't even be in orbit in the solar system.

CHILDREN: It wouldn't. Why not?

EARTH: Because without the pull of gravity from the sun, the Earth would just spin off into space.

(MOON, SUNRISE, SUNSET, *and* EARTH *exit.* CHILDREN *remain on stage with* SUN *and* SUNSPOTS.)

CHILD 6: Wow, I never thought of all those things the sun does for us.

CHILD 7: Yeah, without the sun, nothing would be like it is.

CHILD 8: Nothing would be, period. There would be no life without the sun's heat and light.

CHILD 9: I guess I can stand a little heat wave.

CHILD 1: Yeah, pass the sunscreen and let's celebrate the sun.

The End

ORBIT: how planets travel around the sun

SOLAR SYSTEM: ours includes the sun and all that revolves around it

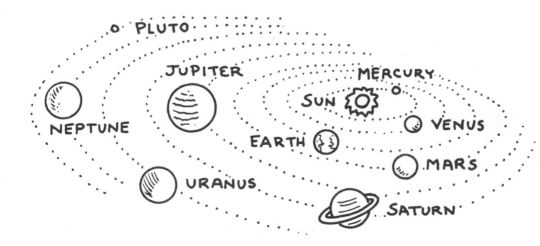

TEACHER'S NOTES

PERFORM IT

Costume this play simply. Child actors wear regular school clothes. The Sun, Sunspots, Earth, and Moon can wear posterboard circles decorated in appropriate colors and labeled "Sun," etc. Plants can wear green clothing. Fossil Fuels can wear black clothing. Sunrise and Sunset can wear no-sew tunics in appropriate colors. Animals can carry large posterboard masks on sticks.

You can lengthen this play performance in several ways. You can open the play by having children recite or read sun facts that they have researched or that you studied in class. Each child who speaks states one fact about the sun. You can close the play by singing one or more songs that use the sun as a theme or metaphor. Some examples are old rock 'n' roll melodies such as "Here Comes the Sun" and "Aquarius/Let the Sun Shine."

This play can be used as a seasonal play to celebrate the arrival of summer. It can also be used as a science-themed play in conjunction with studies of the solar system, plant life cycles, fossils, and food chains. The subject matter covered in the play is basic curriculum study for elementary school children. Depending upon the children's ages, they will be familiar with some or all of the information. The play allows you a creative way to teach some of the subject matter or, in the alternative, to reinforce it.

WRITE IT

As a writing activity, have children create sun poems or sun fact art. To write a sun poem, the child draws a circle for the body of the sun and rays emanating from that circle. On the circle, the child writes the word "sun" or a general sentence about the sun (e.g., The sun warms our world./The sun is important to us.). On each ray, the child writes either an adjective that describes the sun (e.g., hot, yellow, bright, glittery, strong, big) or a sun fact sentence (e.g., Sunspots are cool spots on the sun./The sun has a corona./The sun is made of hydrogen gas.). The type of writing you choose for your sun-writing activity will depend upon the age and sophistication of your students.

EXPLORE IT

If you are doing this play with older children, have them work together in groups with each group creating a large sun poster or diagram. Ask younger students to work in groups, but have each child create a smaller poster of his or her own. Each group will have responsibility for exploring some aspect of the sun.

30

Examples are: sun's location in the solar system and distance from Earth; solar flares; sunspots; sun's corona; sun's hydrogen composition and temperature; sun as a star. Display posters around the room. You can even use them in conjunction with a sun fact presentation at your play performance.

Alternatively, you may ask children to make dioramas about some factual aspect of the sun or about mythical or traditional stories about the sun that you read aloud to them. Such stories include the Daedelus and Icarus legend. Or they could make a diorama about some part of *The Magic School Bus* story referred to in "Read About It."

READ ABOUT IT

Barrett, N. S. *Sun and Stars.* Franklin Watts, 1985.

Cole, Joanna. *The Magic School Bus Lost in the Solar System.* Scholastic, 1990.

Gibbons, Gail. *From Seed to Plant.* Holiday House, 1991.

Krupp, E. C. *The Moon and You.* Macmillan, 1993.

Petty, Kate. *The Sun.* Franklin Watts, 1985.

Stevenson, Robert Louis. *The Moon.* HarperTrophy, 1984.

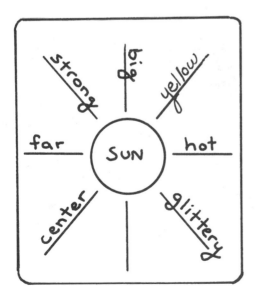

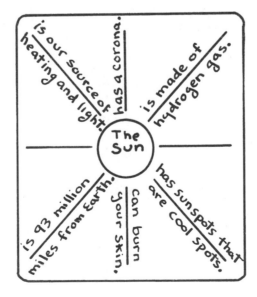

CHAPTER TWO

CELEBRATING
THE WINTER
HOLIDAYS

WINTER IN RHYMELAND

PLAYERS

RHYMELAND CHILDREN 1–21	OLD KING COLE
NARRATOR	MARY CONTRARY
MOTHER GOOSE	WEE WILLIE WINKIE
JACK HORNER	OLD WOMAN IN A SHOE
MISS MUFFET	GOOSE

Teacher's Notes
Begin on
Page 42

SCRIPT

As the play opens, NARRATOR, RHYMELAND CHILDREN, *and*
MOTHER GOOSE *are on stage.* NARRATOR *is to the side.* MOTHER
GOOSE *is at center.* CHILDREN *are placed around the stage. If
you have steps or risers, place* CHILDREN *on steps.*

CHILDREN 14–21: Old Mother Goose
When she wanted to wander
Would ride through the air
On a very fine gander

NARRATOR: Until one day, the day of the great winter festival in
Rhymeland, the goose was gone! When the Children of
Rhymeland heard the news, they were very upset.

ALL CHILDREN: Mother Goose, Mother Goose,
Is it party time today?
The sky is drear. The winter's here.
Is it time for winter play?

MOTHER GOOSE: No, no, we cannot play as yet.
My goose is lost and so I fret.
We cannot have our holiday cheer
'Til we find goose and bring it here.

DREAR: cloudy

FRET: worry

CHEER: happy time

GANDER: full-grown male goose

CHILDREN 14–21 (*sounding upset and concerned*):
> Goosey, goosey gander
> Where did you wander?
> So far from home
> Are you all alone?

CHILD 1 (*pointing to entering actor*): Maybe Jack Horner knows.
> (*Enter* JACK HORNER.)

JACK HORNER: I'm little Jack Horner
> I sat in a corner
> Eating holiday pie
> I put in my thumb
> And pulled out a plum
> What a good boy am I!

CHILD 2: But, Jack Horner, from your corner
> Did a goose you see?

JACK HORNER: Oh no, not me.
> Farewell to thee.
> (*Exit* JACK HORNER.)

CHILDREN 14–21: Goosey, goosey gander
> Where did you wander?
> So far from home
> Are you all alone?

CHILD 3 (*pointing to entering actor*):
> Maybe Miss Muffet knows.
> (*Enter* MISS MUFFET.)

FAREWELL: good-bye

THEE: the person to whom you are speaking

36

From *Take A Quick Bow!*, published by Good Year Books. Copyright © 1997 Pamela Marx.

MISS MUFFET: I'm little Miss Muffet
I sat on a tuffet,
Eating curds and whey.
Along came a spider
Who sat down beside me
And frightened me away.

CHILD 4: But, Miss Muffet, from your tuffet
Did a goose you see?

MISS MUFFET: Oh, no, not me.
Farewell to thee.
(*Exit* MISS MUFFET.)

CHILDREN 14–21: Goosey, goosey gander
Where did you wander?
So far from home
Are you all alone?

CHILD 5 (*pointing to entering actor*): Maybe Old King
Cole knows.
(*Enter* OLD KING COLE.)

OLD KING COLE: I'm Old King Cole.
I'm a merry old soul.
A merry old soul, that's me.
I call for a fife and I call for a drum
And I call for my fiddlers three.

CHILD 6: But, Old King Cole, from your throne
Did a goose you see?

TUFFET: a short stool

CURDS: lumpy, thickened milk—often used to make cheese

WHEY: watery part of curdled milk

FIFE: small flute with a high tone

FIDDLER: violin player

OLD KING COLE: Oh no, not me.
Farewell to thee.
(*Exit* OLD KING COLE.)

CHILDREN 14–21: Goosey, goosey gander
Where did you wander?
So far from home
Are you all alone?

CHILD 7 (*pointing to entering actor*): Maybe Mary Contrary knows.
(*Enter* MARY CONTRARY.)

MARY: I'm Mary Mary Quite Contrary
How does my garden grow?
With silver bells and cockle shells
And pretty maids all in a row.

CHILD 8: But, Mary Contrary, in your garden
Did a goose you see?

MARY: Oh no, not me.
Farewell to thee.
(*Exit* MARY CONTRARY.)

CHILDREN 14–21: Goosey, goosey gander
Where did you wander?
So far from home
Are you all alone?

CHILD 9 (*pointing to entering actor*): Maybe Wee Willie Winkie knows.
(*Enter* WEE WILLIE WINKIE.)

COCKLE SHELL: a kind of seashell

38

WILLIE: I'm Wee Willie Winkie.

I run through the town

Upstairs and downstairs

In my nightgown.

CHILD 10: But, Wee Willie Winkie, on the stairs

Did a goose you see?

WILLIE: Oh no, not me.

Farewell to thee.

(*Exit* WEE WILLIE WINKIE.)

CHILDREN 14–21: Goosey, goosey gander

Where did you wander?

So far from home

Are you all alone?

CHILD 11 (*pointing to entering actor*): Maybe the Old Woman in a Shoe

knows.

(*Enter* OLD WOMAN IN A SHOE.)

OLD WOMAN IN A SHOE: I'm the old woman who lives in a shoe.

I have so many children I don't know what to do.

CHILD 12: But, Old Woman, in your shoe

Did a goose you see?

OLD WOMAN IN A SHOE: Oh no, not me.

Farewell to thee.

(*Exit* OLD WOMAN IN A SHOE. MOTHER GOOSE

starts to cry.)

39

MOTHER GOOSE: Boo hoo, boo hoo
What will I do?

CHILDREN 14–21 *(dramatically):* Boo hoo, boo hoo
What will she do?

CHILD 13: Oh, Mother Goose, you must not cry.
Goose will come back, by and by.
(GOOSE *enters carrying coat, hat, and umbrella. He/she looks
neat and acts unconcerned.*)

GOOSE *(with a superior air):* The north wind doth blow
And we shall have snow
And what will poor goosey do then?

CHILDREN 14–21: Goosey, goosey gander
Where did you wander?

40

GOOSE: Why I've been round the mulberry bush
The mulberry bush, the mulberry bush
I've been round the mulberry bush
All on a frosty morning.
And I found my coat. I found my hat
Tell me, where's the problem in that?
(MOTHER GOOSE *and* CHILDREN *shake heads, shrug shoulders,
and then smile.*)

ALL CHILDREN: Mother Goose, Mother Goose
Gander's no more on the loose.
Is it time for us to meet
For party games and winter treats?

MOTHER GOOSE: Children, yes, the time is here
To celebrate both far and near.

ALL PLAYERS: Fresh October brings the pheasant.
Then to gather nuts is pleasant.
Dull November brings the blast.
Then the leaves are whirling fast.
Chill December's snow and sleet.
Bring blazing fire and winter treat.

The End

MULBERRY BUSH: a tree that bears dark purple fruit

PHEASANT: brightly colored, long-tailed bird

TEACHER'S NOTES

PERFORM IT

Costumes for this play can be done several ways. Rhymeland Children can dress in either robes and/or pajamas carrying stuffed animals or in standard black and white stage clothing, perhaps with hats, aprons, suspenders, and other accessories, as appropriate. Specific characters should wear clothing appropriate to characters: Mother Goose and Old Woman in a Shoe—long skirts, aprons, and granny caps or paper bonnets; Miss Muffet and Mary Contrary—long skirts, aprons and ruffles, or fancy old-fashioned little girl dresses; Jack Horner and Goose—black and white stage clothing with tie and suspenders; Old King Cole—black and white stage clothing, red cape, and paper crown; and Wee Willie Winkie—nightshirt or pajamas.

You can easily extend this performance with songs. For younger children you can both precede and follow the play with one or more nursery rhyme songs. Song sources are *Mickey's Favorite Children's Songs* published by The Big 3 Music Corporation (1979) or *The Great Big Book of Children's Songs* published by Hal Leonard Corporation (1995). In the alternative, different Mother Goose rhymes can be humorously recited and pantomimed before the play begins. At the end of the play, you might close with a traditional winter song such as "Jingle Bells" or "Winter Wonderland."

To prepare children for this play, read them the complete Mother Goose rhymes for each of the characters in the play. Have them think about some of the silly (e.g., Mary Contrary grows bells and shells) and realistic (e.g., Old Woman has many children and little money) aspects of the rhymes. Explain that these rhymes come from written and oral storytelling traditions and have been shared with children over many generations. Many rhymes originated in the British Isles as part of the English storytelling tradition.

WRITE IT

Have children pick a Mother Goose rhyme of their choice from any standard collection. The child reads his or her poem and then writes a story about "and then what happened?" In other words, each child writes a short story about what happens to the character(s) after the poem ends. This can be used as a journal writing exercise if you choose.

For younger children, have them

choose one of the Mother Goose characters from the play. Ask them to draw a simple picture of the character and then describe the character in three sentences.

Example:

This is Mary Quite Contrary.
She has a garden.
She grows silver bells.

EXPLORE IT

Children can make coat hanger people of their favorite nursery rhyme characters. You can use these to decorate your room. They can even be presented before the play along with reading/recitation of the related poem. After you have finished with classroom use of the coat hanger people, check with the local school or city librarian to see if they might be displayed in another location.

READ ABOUT IT

Langstaff, Nancy, and John Langstaff, comp. *Jim Along, Josie: A Collection of Folk Songs and Singing Games for Young Children.* Harcourt Brace Jovanovich, 1970.

Emerson, Sally, comp. *The Kingfisher Nursery Rhyme Songbook.* Kingfisher, 1992

For cross-cultural rhymes to share with class, consider:

Delacre, Lulu, sel. *Arroz Con Leche: Popular Songs and Rhymes from Latin America.* Scholastic, 1989.

Griego, Margot; Betsy Bucks; Sharon Gilbert; and Laurel Kimball. *Tortellitas Para Mama.* Holt, 1981.

Wyndham, Robert, ed. *Chinese Mother Goose Rhymes.* Philomel Books, 1989.

THE MAGIC TOY SHOP

PLAYERS

SHOPKEEPER

TOYS 1–3

STUFFED ANIMALS 1–6

WIND-UPS 1–5

BALLS 1–5

SPINNING TOPS 1–5

YO-YOS 1–5

Teacher's Notes Begin on Page 50

SCRIPT

Shopkeeper moves among TOYS 1–3 *and* STUFFED ANIMALS 1–6, *whose heads are down and eyes are closed. He/she may hold a duster and dust at them occasionally as one might at the end of a day. The* TOYS *and* STUFFED ANIMALS *stand and sit randomly around the stage. Toys may be toy soldiers, ballerinas, dolls, rocking horses, airplanes, or any combination of other toys for which students have costumes.*

SHOPKEEPER: Well, my little toy friends, it is the end of another busy day. Lights off. Doors locked. Sleep well until tomorrow. *(He exits.)*

STUFFED ANIMAL 1 *(lifts head with eyes wide open):* Sleep well! How can I sleep? How will I find out? What is the answer? What does it all mean?

(Other toys begin to wake up, open their eyes, and stretch.)

TOY 1: What is your problem?

TOY 2: Yeah. Why are you playing "20 Questions" in the middle of the night?

TOY 1: I don't understand. Why are you upset? You've got it made.

TOY 2: That's right. You all have the best "toy" job around. People love stuffed animals.

TOY 3: Yes. They hug you and take care of you. What could be better?

"20 QUESTIONS": a party game where players ask up to 20 questions before guessing the answer

STUFFED ANIMAL 1: I know. I know. But what's the point of it all?

STUFFED ANIMAL 2: Yeah. Our fur gets worn. We get patchy and ugly and then we're forgotten.

STUFFED ANIMAL 3: You wait and see. Like he/she said. What's the point?
(*Enter the* WIND-UPS.)

WIND-UP 1: Listen, you have nothing to complain about. Look at us. There is no point to what we do at all.

WIND-UP 2: We wait and wait and wait for someone to wind us up. And when they do, we just go in circles like this.
(*Several* WIND-UPS *demonstrate by walking robotically in circles. This could be done to music or some percussion and bell rhythm that children make with classroom percussion instruments.*)

WIND-UP 3: So we go in a circle as-fast-as-we-can (*getting slower, voice getting lower*). And—then—we—wind—d-o-w-n (*stops moving*).

WIND-UP 4: Again and again and again—we go in our circles. No matter what we do, we never get anywhere.

WIND-UP 5: You know, that's true, but . . . (*stops to think for a moment*) I always enjoy hearing the child who wound me up laugh as I strut about.

WIND-UP 3: You know, you're right. A child's laughter always makes me feel good too.

WIND-UP 2: Yes, a smile can make almost anything worthwhile.
(WIND-UPS *exit smiling, shaking heads, and talking to one another.*)

STRUT: to walk with pride

46

STUFFED ANIMAL 4: Well, I don't know if that's really enough to give a toy's life meaning.
(*Enter* BALLS.)

BALL 1: You don't know? Think about us. We never know what's going to happen when someone picks us up.

BALL 2: Will we get hit with a racket? or smacked with a bat? or bounced on the asphalt?

BALL 3: Yeah, talk about painful jobs.

BALL 4: It's pretty hard to worry about the meaning of life when you're bouncing, bouncing, bouncing on your head all day.

BALL 5: It can be such a headache. On the other hand, when children play with us, they get exercise and laugh and run.

BALL 3: And when they play baseball or basketball or soccer, they learn about teamwork and cooperation.

BALL 4: I do enjoy being part of a team.
(BALLS *exit, shaking heads "yes" and talking among themselves.*)

STUFFED ANIMAL 5: Oh, I don't know if that's really enough.
(*Enter* TOPS.)

TOP 1 (*emphasizing the word "big" with a sarcastic tone*): You don't know. You don't know. You all think you've got such big problems.

TOP 2: Think about spinning until your eyes pop out.

TOP 3: Yes, that's a top's life. Spinning and spinning and spinning. Really fun, huh?

TOP 4: On the other hand, everyone loves a top. We're just plain simple fun.

RACKET: a special paddle for hitting balls

ASPHALT: a tar mixed with pebbles and used to cover roads

MEANING OF LIFE: a thinker's questions about why people or animals live and work as they do

47

TOP 5: Yes. Everyone likes to see how long and how fast they can spin us.

TOP 4: Yes. I like all the attention, and someone is having fun at the same time.

TOP 3: Not a bad life, really, is it?

(TOPS *exit, shaking heads "yes," and* YO-YOS *enter.*)

STUFFED ANIMAL 6: You think it's enough just to make someone smile once in a while? I'm still not sure. . . .

YO-YO 1: Oh, brother. You are so whiny. Look at us.

YO-YO 2: All we do is roll down and up, down and up, down and up. And you don't see us complaining.

YO-YO 3: When a child plays with us, they work hard to learn how to use us.

YO-YO 4: And how to do tricks with us. They are so proud when they succeed because they have done it all themselves.

YO-YO 3: You should see their big smiles.

YO-YO 5 *(very sure):* Of course it's all worthwhile. A smile, a laugh— they are what life is all about.

STUFFED ANIMAL 3: You are all right. A chance to make someone happy is important.

STUFFED ANIMAL 4: Yes, it's about the most important thing there is in life.

WORTHWHILE:
being of value for the time spent

STUFFED ANIMAL 5 *(with relief):* And it's even better since we don't have to be hit with rackets and bounced on our heads.

STUFFED ANIMAL 6: Oh, I hope someone takes me home to a child tomorrow so I can make someone smile.

ALL TOYS *(sort of dreamily):* Oh yes. I hope, I hope, I hope. *(And as the* TOYS *say these lines they close their eyes, put their heads down, and then the lights fade out.)*

The End

TEACHER'S NOTES

PERFORM IT

Consider these costume ideas for this play. The Shopkeeper can wear the basic black and white stage attire with an apron. Old Halloween costumes and dance attire are a great source of costumes for the assorted Toys and Stuffed Animals. (Any animal costumes will do.) If animal costumes are in short supply, supplement with paper ears on headbands, face paint, and attire in the appropriate color. Wind-ups can all dress in the same color with hats of some sort, or the standard black and white dress; add posterboard turnkeys for their backs. Balls, Tops, and Yo-yos can all wear black and white stage clothing with brightly colored, appropriate toy shapes cut out of posterboard and tied around their necks. In the alternative, Balls can simply carry large balls.

You can expand the presentation of this play in several ways. You can close the play with one or more holiday songs that celebrate toys. These include "Jolly Old St. Nicholas" and "Toyland" (by Victor Herbert).

To prepare children for this play, you might consider the following activity, which can also be performed in conjunction with the play, if you choose. Consider involving children in pantomiming toy activities to a segment of Tchaikovsky's *The Nutcracker.* Appropriate dance segments include "Dance of the Sugar Plum Fairy" and "Waltz of the Flowers." For the pantomime, ask two children to act as mischievous toymaker's elves. The other children pantomime the movements of wind-up toys of their choice. The toys are randomly located about the room or stage. To the chosen music, the elves mischievously run from toy to toy, winding each up and giggling as they go. Once wound, the toys wake up and perform their repetitive movements to the music and then wind down as the music fades, and the elves yawn and fall asleep.

This short stage piece is easy, fun for the children, and allows for the easy introduction of classical music and composers—Tchaikovsky being a Russian composer of the Romantic period. As you do this pantomime activity, tell children that *The Nutcracker* is a famous ballet, especially popular at Christmas. It is the story of a girl named Clara who receives for Christmas a nutcracker that is later broken by her brother. She falls asleep and dreams of princes and mouse kings and fairies.

WRITE IT

Children might enjoy writing a "biography" of a favorite stuffed animal. If you do the measurement activities listed below, this information can be included. These biographies are fantasy, of course, so encourage children to be creative about the birth, life, and adventures of their toys.

A simpler writing activity is to have children make a toy triangle. They draw a toy inside a triangle. At each corner of the triangle, they write about the toy. At one corner, they write the type of toy (e.g., doll, ball, airplane). At the second corner, they write three adjectives describing its appearance, and at the third corner, they write three verbs describing what it does.

Examples:

Ball
Round, orange, smooth
Bounces, rolls, stops

Teddy bear
Soft, brown, cuddly
Sits, looks, leans

EXPLORE IT

Hold a Stuffed Animal or Teddy Bear Day by having each child bring a favorite stuffed animal to school. As part of the day's festivities, do some teddy bear math. With string and rulers, you can have children measure the overall height of the toy, the waist, arm length, and leg length. If children can, have them convert some or all of the measurements from metric to U.S. customary or vice versa. You can also do one or more class graphs of the toy's colors, species, and the like. As a related activity, have children estimate, count, sort, and graph the colors of snack-sized gummy bear candy packs, as well as find out costs of candy packets and individual gummies based upon overall package costs. Finally, have a teddy bear picnic. For this part of the day, children bring favorite "bear foods" to school—bear claws, honey cake, cookies or bread, tuna fish sandwiches (real bears like fish), and similar foods.

READ ABOUT IT

Any available version of the Pinocchio story works well as a read-aloud activity with this play.

Degen, Bruce. *Jamberry.* Harper & Row, 1983.

Hoban, Russell. *The Mouse and His Child.* Harper & Row, 1967. (For reading aloud)

Simon, Carly. *Amy the Dancing Bear.* Doubleday, 1989.

Williams, Margery. *The Velveteen Rabbit.* Julian Messner, 1993.

51

THE MAGIC HOLIDAY DICTIONARY

Dragon
Diwali
First Footer
Junkanoo
Soba Noodle

PLAYERS

CHILDREN 1–6	SCOTLAND 1–3
JAPAN 1–4	CHINA 1–6
BAHAMAS 1–6	INDIA 1–5

Teacher's Notes Begin on Page 58

SCRIPT

As the play opens, a large book (the dictionary) is propped up in the center of the stage. It can be made out of pieces of posterboard and decorated to look like a book. It should have several posterboard pages that can be turned. CHILDREN 1–6 *gather around the book.*

CHILD 1: This is an interesting dictionary. It's a dictionary of holiday words, isn't it?

CHILD 2: Yes. And mostly it's about New Year holidays.

CHILD 3: We thought this book might help us come up with some new ideas for our New Year party.

CHILD 4: That sounds like fun.

CHILD 5: Look! Here's a phrase I haven't heard before. I wonder what New Year custom it is about.

CHILD 6: What's the phrase?

CHILD 4: It's "soba noodle."

(As children say the words "soba noodle," use some lighting effect to signal that something unusual is happening. The effect can be achieved by flashing stage lights or turning stage lights down or off and having several children with flashlights move their light beams in circles around the stage. This goes on for only a few seconds—perhaps enough time to get actors onto the stage—and then the stage lights return to normal.

CUSTOM: a practice used over time by a group of people

53

While the effect is underway, JAPAN 1–4 *enter. They are in the middle of a discussion. All players hold small bowls.)*

JAPAN 1: Oh, we just love soba noodles and hot soup for New Year here in Japan. *(Players look into each other's bowls.)*

JAPAN 2: Boy, I think you have the longest soba noodle of all.

JAPAN 3: If you can swallow it whole in one gulp, you will have very good luck in the new year.

JAPAN 4: It's a long noodle, but I can do it. After all, it's for good luck. *(Lighting effect occurs and* JAPAN 1–4 *exit.)*

CHILD 1: Did you see that? What happened here?

CHILD 2: It's almost like the dictionary came alive.

CHILD 3: Turn the pages and pick another word. Let's see what happens.

CHILD 4: Here's a word. It's "Junkanoo."
(The same lighting effect occurs as before. While it occurs, BAHAMAS 1–6 *enter. They wear brightly colored clothes with streamers and fancy hats. Play calypso music as background.)*

BAHAMAS 1: You have a beautiful costume this year for the Bahamas' Junkanoo parade.

BAHAMAS 2 *(displaying colorful skirt or shirt):* Yes, I wanted to have every color of the rainbow in my costume.

BAHAMAS 3: Junkanoo is my favorite holiday. I love all the festivals and dancing and parades.

BAHAMAS 4: It's a great way to celebrate the new year.

BAHAMAS 5: My teacher told me there is a legend about a hero named Johnny Canoe visiting the Bahamas.

BAHAMAS 6: I've heard that too. That's how Junkanoo began.
(Lighting effect occurs and BAHAMAS 1–6 *exit.)*

CHILD 1: Amazing!

CHILD 2: Let's do it again. Pick another word or phrase.

CHILD 3: Yes, this is a great way to learn about New Year customs around the world.

CHILD 4 *(looking through book and pointing):* Okay, the word is "first-footer."

CHILD 5: Here we go again.
(Lighting effect occurs and SCOTLAND 1–3 *enter.* SCOTLAND 1–3 *all stand together as though looking at the door.)*

SCOTLAND 1: It's midnight. The first minute of the new year has arrived here in Scotland.

SCOTLAND 2: I wonder who the first person to come through our door will be.

SCOTLAND 3: I hope it's someone friendly and nice. That kind of first-footer would bring us luck for the new year for sure.
(Lighting effect occurs and SCOTLAND 1–3 *exit.)*

CHILD 1: Amazing!

CHILD 2: Let's do it again.

CHILD 3: Pick a word.

CHILD 6 *(looking through book and pointing):* The word is "Diwali."

CHILD 5: Here we go again.
(Lighting effect occurs and INDIA 1–5 *enter carrying small clay lamps.)*

55

INDIA 1: I love all the lighted lamps at our Diwali New Year celebration.

INDIA 2: Yes, Diwali is a beautiful celebration here in India.

INDIA 3: It's just about my favorite holiday.

INDIA 4: Well, all this talk is fine, but let's put out our lamps.

INDIA 5: I'm with you. Until we set them out, we can't light them. And until we light them, we can't eat.
(Lighting effect occurs and INDIA *1–5 exit.)*

CHILD 1: Amazing!

CHILD 2: Let's do it just one more time. Please!

CHILD 3: Pick a word.

CHILD 4 *(looking through book and pointing):* The word is "dragon."

CHILD 5: Here we go again.
(Lighting effect occurs and CHINA *1–6 enter carrying dragon head made from posterboard and decorated with red and gold streamers.)*

CHINA 1: This is my favorite part of our New Year celebration here in China.

CHINA 2: And our Chinese New Year celebration has everything—food, parties. . . .

CHINA 3: And presents too. Mine are always wrapped in red paper.

CHINA 4: Well, it's time to get ready for the dragon parade.

CHINA 5: Yes, line up. I'll hold the head.

CHINA 6: Well, here we go. Remember to move up and down so we look like a real dragon.
(When the dragon is ready, actors snake around stage with the dragon head. Offstage actors can beat pots and pans while the dragon snakes around the stage.)

56

CHINA 1–6: Gung Hay Fat Choy!

> *(Dragon parade moves offstage in parade formation. Lighting effect occurs, as* CHINA 1–6 *exit with dragon prop and banging stops.)*

CHILD 1: This is the best book I've ever read.

CHILD 2: It sure taught me a lot about New Year customs around the world.

CHILD 3: I'd like to use some of these customs in my own New Year celebrations.

CHILD 4: Around the world, New Year is a time to look to the future.

CHILD 5: And looking to the future is always reason to celebrate.

CHILD 6: Yes, we all look forward to a happy and prosperous new year.

> *(All actors reenter stage. The next lines are said by actors in unison, or you can have half the group speak the first line, half the group speak the second line, and the whole group speak the last line. As an even better alternative, have children as a class write their own closing lines to say here.)*

PROSPEROUS: having enough money and comforts

ALL ACTORS: Whenever you celebrate New Year

In whatever way you celebrate it

May your New Year wishes come true.

The End

57

TEACHER'S NOTES

PERFORM IT

Costumes for this play, with the exception of Children 1–6, begin with the basic black and white stage attire. Children 1–6 can wear regular school clothes. Work to provide ethnic accents to the other actors' basic attire. For the Japan and China actors, basic clothing can be accented with kimono jackets, Chinese pajamas, and the like. Accent the Scotland actors with plaid vests, caps, skirts, and sashes as available. The Bahamas actors can wear brightly colored sashes, skirts, paper vests, shirts, and paper hats. One child should have a "rainbow" skirt or shirt. This can be accomplished by letting crepe paper streamers hang from the waistband of a brightly colored skirt or from a pipe cleaner necklace hung with multi-colored paper streamers. India actors can be accented with Indian scarves or sashes as appropriate.

One way to add a brief segment to the end of the play is to have different children find out how to say "Happy New Year" in different languages and have them say those phrases after the final lines of the play.

Another play extender is to pick

songs from one or more of the countries or regions indicated in the play (i.e., the Caribbean, China, Japan, India, and Scotland) and have children sing several international songs. Several international songbook resources are:

Gritton, Peter. *Folksongs from the Far East.* Faber Music, 1991.
Mickey's Favorite Children's Songs. The Big 3 Music Corporation, 1979.
Silverman, Jerry. *Children Sing Around the World.* Mel Bay Publications, Inc., 1991.

You could also have children sing "It's a Small World" as a closing song.

To prepare children for this play, talk to them a little about New Year around the world and specifically the customs noted in the play. New Year celebrations occur around the year. Jewish New Year (Rosh Hashanah) and Indian Diwali occur in the fall. Scottish Hogmanay and Japanese New Year occur January 1. Bahaman Junkanoo occurs the week leading up to January 1. Chinese New Year occurs in mid-winter.

Here are some brief facts about well-known New Year celebrations, including those in the play:

Diwali—In India, there are many dif-

ferent New Year celebrations. Diwali, also called the festival of lights, is perhaps the most spectacular. It is a Hindu festival occurring in October or November. Diwali marks the victory of good over evil. Tiny clay lamps or saucers called *dipas* are filled with oil and a wick and lit. By legend, Lakshmi (goddess of prosperity) returns to the plains from the hills on Diwali. The dipas light her way, and she blesses lit homes.

Hogmanay—This is Scottish New Year. Houses are cleaned and foods like oatmeal cakes, black buns (spiced cakes with nuts and raisins), and scones are eaten. On Hogmanay Eve, families hold open houses for friends and relatives. The first person at midnight to enter the house signifies luck for the new year.

Japanese New Year—At Japanese New Year on January 1, people stack rice cakes, called *mochi,* for good luck. People also eat mochi. Children fly kites and eat soba noodles with broth. Swallowing a long noodle whole means good luck.

Junkanoo—The Bahaman celebration occurs right before January 1 and includes feasting, parades, and dancing. The holiday's name is adapted from a legendary hero, Johnny Canoe, who wore brightly colored, tattered clothes.

Chinese New Year—Central to the multi-day New Year celebrations are the Lion and Dragon parades. Families get together for feasting and give small gifts, often wrapped in red paper.

Rosh Hashanah—The Jewish New Year occurs in the fall as part of the Jewish high holy days. Apples and challah (bread) are dipped in honey to signify a sweet new year. Since this is a religious festival, services are held and begin with the blowing of the shofar, or ram's horn.

WRITE IT

Writing New Year resolutions is a straight-forward writing activity that you can use to lead children in different directions. Ask children to think about things around them that they believe need change. These things can be about themselves, their schools and family, their community, their country, and the world. Ask them to pick three of these subjects and write resolutions for the new year explaining what they personally intend to do about each of them.

Example:

I resolve for myself this new year to read more books.

I resolve for my community this new year to pick up litter.

I resolve for my world this new year to always recycle.

EXPLORE IT

This play lends itself well to several multicultural crafts, some of which can be

59

used as play props. Making small Diwali lamps from clay is fun. Find a picture of a Diwali lamp in a resource book at your local library so children can use it for inspiration. Once the lamp is shaped, let it dry and glue in a string wick.

A craft taken from Chinese tradition is a New Year greeting banner. Find books with Chinese character lettering for children to imitate. Use cotton swabs and black paint to draw characters on white paper. Frame the paper in red construction paper and use gold foil pieces, if available, to add drama to the frame. Hang on a piece of red yarn.

If you prefer, use this play as an opportunity to reinforce geography with an oral class game in the style of the TV show *Jeopardy*. For this activity, the teacher makes a statement about places or customs in the play and the children answer back with a question. You can break the class into teams of six students each, and children can work together and even use class maps to get the answers. Game examples are:

Teacher: *This country is on the continent of Asia.*
Children: *What is China?*
Teacher: *This holiday celebrates a folk hero named Johnny Canoe.*
Children: *What is Junkanoo?*

READ ABOUT IT

Behrens, June. *Gung Hay Fat Choy.* Childrens Press, 1982.

Brown, Tricia. *Chinese New Year.* Henry Holt, 1987.

Gilmore, Rachna. *Lights for Gita.* Tibury House Publishers, 1994.

Johnson, Lois S. *Happy New Year Round the World.* Rand McNally & Company, 1966. (Read aloud or background information)

Modell, Frank. *Goodbye Old Year, Hello New Year.* Greenwillow, 1984.

Waters, Kate, and Madeline Slovenz-Low. *Lion Dancer: Ernie Wan's Chinese New Year.* Scholastic, 1990.

A DIFFERENT CHRISTMAS

♪ ♪
Let there
be Peace
on Earth !!
♪

A DIFFERENT CHRISTMAS

PLAYERS

ELVES 1–2
SANTA

GIFT-GIVERS 1–20
CHILDREN 1–7

Teacher's Notes Begin on Page 66

SCRIPT

As the play begins, SANTA *and* ELVES *are situated at top, center stage. This play works best performed on risers. The* GIFT-GIVERS *are located in their groups on risers under* SANTA *and* ELVES *and around* CHILDREN *1–7. If the play is performed on a regular stage, have* SANTA *and* ELVES *at center stage and* CHILDREN *1–7 seated/standing near them as though talking. In the center of* CHILDREN *1–7 is a large posterboard Earth (or papier-mâché Earth made on an over-sized balloon available at science supply stores).*

ELF 1: What is it, Santa? What's wrong?

SANTA: It's strange indeed. The children are not asking for presents this year. They are giving presents instead.

ELF 2: What caused this, Santa?

SANTA: Let's listen and maybe we can find out.
(SANTA *and* ELVES *lean toward children and hold hands up to ears as though trying to hear.*)

CHILD 1: I see a lot of people in our own town who need help.

CHILD 2: And I read stories in magazines about people all over the world who are hungry or sick.

CHILD 3: Our teacher taught us about how the Earth has lots of environmental problems.

CHILD 4: There must be something we can do to help.

CHILD 5: Yes, the holiday season is a good time of year to think about others.

ENVIRONMENTAL: concerning the total surroundings that affect the well-being of living things

63

CHILD 6: But what can we really do about those problems? They are such big problems.

CHILD 7: I'll bet if we think about it, we can come up with something. (CHILDREN *pantomime a continued conversation and thinking, for example, chin resting on hand or scratching head.*)

ELF 1: Look, Santa, here come some more children now.

ELF 2: It looks like they have gifts.

SANTA: Let's listen and see if we can find out what's happening. (SANTA *and* ELVES *lean to listen. Enter/stand* GIFT-GIVERS 1–5; *one carries a symbol of the gift they want to give. Each of the four groups of* GIFT-GIVERS *decides on the gift they as a group want to give the Earth. Three of the five then state lines that the group has made up to explain the gift. Examples are given below.*

The GIFT-GIVERS *pantomime talking among themselves. When* SANTA *and* ELVES *finish their lines, gift-givers begin speaking loudly.*)

GIFT-GIVER 1: Our world needs many things.

GIFT-GIVER 2: I think we can help.

GIFT-GIVERS 3–5 *[These actors state their own lines written by the group about the gift they would choose to give to the world. As examples only:*

- *Many people in the world are hungry.*
  We will help give the gift of food.
  Then people will not be hungry anymore.

- *The world is fighting pollution.*
  We can help plant trees.
  Trees help keep our air clean.]

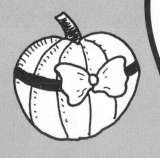

(CHILDREN 1–7 *hold the Earth replica.* GIFT-GIVERS *tape a symbol of their gift to the Earth and exit stage or return to places. Enter/stand* GIFT-GIVERS 6–10 *carrying symbols of gifts.*)

GIFT-GIVER 6: Our world needs many things.

GIFT-GIVER 7: I think we can help.

GIFT-GIVERS 8–10: [GIFT-GIVERS 8–10 *each make a statement about their group's gift to the world.*]
(*One* GIFT-GIVER *affixes symbol of gift to Earth. Exit/sit* GIFT-GIVERS 6–10 *and enter/stand* GIFT-GIVERS 11–15.)

GIFT-GIVER 11: Our world needs many things.

GIFT-GIVER 12: I think we can help.

GIFT-GIVERS 13–15: [*These actors each say a statement concerning their group's gift to the world.*]
(*One* GIFT-GIVER *affixes symbol of gift to Earth prop. Exit/sit* GIFT-GIVERS 11–15 *and enter/stand* GIFT-GIVERS 16–20.)

GIFT-GIVER 16: Our world needs many things.

GIFT-GIVER 17: I think we can help.

GIFT-GIVERS 18–20: [*These actors each say a statement concerning their group's gift to the world.*]
(*One* GIFT-GIVER *affixes a symbol of the gift to the Earth prop. Exit/sit* GIFT-GIVERS 16–20.)

ELF 1: But, Santa, how can children give the world such big gifts?

SANTA: The same way anything big gets done—one step at a time.

ELF 2: This may be the merriest Christmas of all.
(*All actors reenter stage or, if on stage, they stand.*)

The End

TEACHER'S NOTES

PERFORM IT

Costume Santa and his Elves in red and green no-sew tunics, respectively. Santa caps or red and green Robin Hood-type hats are fine accessories. Children can wear nice party clothing. The Gift-Givers should wear ethnic clothing from around the world. Black and white stage clothing can be made to look more international by adding brightly colored waist sashes. Children who do not have ethnic clothing can be American carolers wearing jackets, winter caps, and woolen scarves.

This play should end with one or two songs that all the children sing. Excellent choices that are familiar and easy to learn are "It's a Small World," "I'd Like to Teach the World to Sing," and "Let There Be Peace on Earth." This last song works nicely if the last gift has a peace theme. After one of these songs, you might close with "We Wish You a Merry Christmas," followed by individual children calling out the words "Merry Christmas" in different languages from around the world.

Preparing children for this play is easy. The holiday season is a time of year when discussions about giving come up naturally. Such classroom discussions about giving to others serve to prepare student groups for working together to develop ideas and write lines about gifts they want to give to the world.

WRITE IT

Ask children to imagine that one of the richest people in the world has just volunteered to donate $1 billion to help try to solve a specific world problem. Have children write a simple news article about the gift, the need it fills, and the giver. Ask that children answer the standard journalistic questions—*who, what, where, why, when,* and *how*—as they write their news stories. Children will be using their imaginations as to the name of the billionaire and the details, but can learn about how news stories are structured by looking at the newspaper in class or at home with parents as a homework assignment.

Christmas gift acrostics are another writing possibility. Consider the following types of acrostics: use the word "Christmas" or "holiday" to inspire sentences, or single-word gifts given at the holidays or given to the world.

Examples:

Sentence Acrostic

C Christmas is a time for giving.

H Happiness comes from giving to others.

R Ring in the holiday season by doing a kind deed.

I Is just one kindness to another person enough?

S Selfishness is only thinking about what you want.

T Try to think about others first.

M Many gifts are needed by others and our world.

A Anyone can help out.

S Stars shine brighter when we think of others.

Noun /Noun and Adjective Acrostics

H Hats

O Oranges

L Licorice

I Ice Cream

D Dolls

A Almonds

Y Yo-Yos

C Clean air

H Hopeful thoughts

R Recycling efforts

I Inspiring work

S Selfless dedication

T Tireless conservation

M Many helpers

A Amazing ideas

S Special people

EXPLORE IT

Have children choose a "holiday helpfulness" activity that the class can organize together. Examples are: food drives, sock/mitten collections, recycling drives, bake sales/penny collections to raise money for a worthy cause, making decorative items for a convalescent hospital, and caroling at a home for the disabled or elderly. These activities help children act on the theme of the play at a time of the year when their own "wish lists" are often paramount to them.

READ ABOUT IT

Howard, Tracy Apple. *Kids Ending Hunger.* Andrews & McMeel, 1992. (Classroom resource)

Silverstein, Shel. *The Giving Tree.* Harper & Row, 1964.

Zolotow, Charlotte. *Mr. Rabbit and the Lovely Present.* HarperTrophy, 1962.

67

EVAN'S CHRISTMAS CAROL

PLAYERS

EVAN (OR EVA)

FRIENDS 1–2

SIBLINGS 1–2

GHOSTS HERE 1–3

GHOSTS THERE 1–3

GHOSTS EVERYWHERE 1–3

PEOPLE 1–16

Teacher's Notes Begin on Page 74

SCRIPT

As the play opens, EVAN *(or* EVA*) and two friends are sitting in the middle of the floor with holiday catalogs and long strips of paper writing holiday wish lists. Three chairs in a row are at the side of the stage.* SIBLINGS *1–2 enter and look disgustedly at this selfish behavior.*

FRIEND 1 *(holding up long list):* Boy, my list is really getting long.

FRIEND 2: I sure hope I get everything I ask for.

EVAN: Will you both be quiet? I still have my list to finish.
(He holds up a very long list.)

SIBLING 1: You know, Evan, presents are not what Christmas is all about.

EVAN: Leave me alone so I can finish.

SIBLING 2: You are such a scrooge. Christmas is a time to think about someone besides yourself for a change.

SIBLING 1: I wonder if you'll ever learn.
*(*SIBLINGS *exit.)*

FRIEND 1: Boy, this list-writing makes you awfully tired.

FRIEND 2: I think we should just rest for a bit.
*(*EVAN *and* FRIENDS *1–2 move to three chairs lined up at side of stage. As soon as they sit down, they drop their heads onto*

SCROOGE: a stingy person—from the Charles Dickens character, Ebenezer Scrooge

their shoulders as though asleep. This should be done at the same time for effect, with all heads falling on the right or left shoulder as agreed.)
(Enter GHOSTS HERE *1–3.)*

GHOST HERE 1 *(acting spooky while waving arms like a ghost):* Children. Children.

*(*EVAN *and* FRIENDS *raise heads at the same time and look alert and a little frightened.)*

EVAN: Who are you? Why are you here?

GHOST HERE 2: We are the Ghosts of Christmas Here. We're here, children, because you need to see something.

*(*GHOSTS *wave hands and* PERSONS *1–8 enter. They re-create the scene of a soup kitchen.* GHOSTS *move to side of stage or exit briefly during scene.)*

PERSON 1 *(pointing to one side as though to a line of hungry people):* We have all these people to feed.

PERSON 2: Yes, there is still a long line of people waiting to be fed.

PERSON 3: How are we going to feed them all?

PERSON 4: I'm afraid our food might run out.

PERSON 5: There never seems to be enough food.

PERSON 6: Why can't just a few more people think about those who are in need in our community?

PERSON 7: If they thought about it, I'm sure they would donate some food to help.

PERSON 8: Well, we just have to keep on trying.

*(*PEOPLE *1–8 exit.* GHOSTS HERE *come back to center stage.)*

EVAN *(amazed, but troubled):* Wow, there are people in our town who have to wait in line for food!

COMMUNITY: a group of people who live together in a place

70

FRIEND 1: That's terrible.

FRIEND 2: Somebody ought to do something.

GHOST HERE 3: Yes, children, somebody ought to.
(GHOSTS HERE 1–3 *exit. As they leave,* EVAN *and* FRIENDS *immediately put their heads on shoulders at the same time with eyes closed as though asleep. Enter* GHOSTS THERE 1–3.)

GHOST THERE 1 (*acting spooky while waving arms*): Children. Children.
(EVAN *and* FRIENDS *raise heads at the same time and look alert.*)

GHOST THERE 2: We are the Ghosts of Christmas There.

GHOST THERE 3 (*pointing to entering actors*): Look over there, children. Not everyone lives in a nice warm home with a big warm coat, hat, and mittens.
(GHOSTS THERE 1–3 *exit or go to side of stage while* PERSONS 9–16 *enter.*)

PERSON 9 (*shivering*): It's so cold this winter.

PERSON 10 (*shivering*): I can't remember a winter that has been this cold.

PERSON 11 (*shivering*): Do you think this cold snap will ever end?

PERSON 12: I wish I had some mittens. My fingers are freezing.

PERSON 13: I need some warm socks. I can't even feel my toes anymore.

PERSON 14 (*holding a doll as a child*): And a hat. I need a hat and mittens for my child.

PERSON 15: Well, maybe it will warm up soon.

PERSON 16: I don't know what we will do if it doesn't warm up at least a little bit.
(*Exit* PERSONS 9–16. GHOSTS THERE 1–3 *enter to center stage.*)

71

FRIEND 1: How awful to be cold and shivery all winter!

EVAN: It's terrible!

FRIEND 2: Somebody ought to do something.

GHOST THERE 3: Yes, children, somebody ought to.
      (GHOSTS THERE 1–3 *exit. As they do,* EVAN *and* FRIENDS *put their heads on shoulders and close eyes as though asleep. Enter* GHOSTS EVERYWHERE 1–3.)

GHOST EVERYWHERE 1 *(acting spooky while waving arms):* Children. Children.
      (EVAN *and* FRIENDS *raise heads and look alert.*)

GHOST EVERYWHERE 2: We're the Ghosts of Christmas Everywhere.

GHOST EVERYWHERE 3: Have you learned anything today, children?

EVAN: Yes, we just didn't realize how lucky we are.

FRIEND 1: We have plenty of food to eat . . .

FRIEND 2: And warm clothes and a home.

GHOST EVERYWHERE 1: Yes, children, there are people who are in need in your community.

GHOST EVERYWHERE 2: And in other parts of the country and around the world.

GHOST EVERYWHERE 3: Christmas is a time to make wishes not only for ourselves, but for all those people as well.

EVAN: We know that now, and we can do some things to help. We can take food to the food drive at school.

FRIEND 1: And we can collect mittens for a mitten tree at city hall.

FRIEND 2: And we can go caroling to people who can't get out very much.

GHOSTS EVERYWHERE 1–3: What would you sing?

EVAN: I know a great song . . .

(Enter all actors. Entire class sings "Let There Be Peace on Earth," "I'd Like to Teach the World to Sing," "Everywhere, Everywhere Christmas Tonight," "We Wish You a Merry Christmas," or "It's a Small World.")

The End

TEACHER'S NOTES

PERFORM IT

Evan, Siblings, and Friends can all wear regular school clothes as costumes. The Ghosts can wear all white or the black and white stage clothing with white net ponchos hanging from their shoulders. The food kitchen actors can wear aprons over regular clothes. The actors portraying needy people can wear old, worn clothing, perhaps with patches and holes at the knees.

This play is based upon a book steeped in English holiday traditions, and the script challenges children to look to the larger world and the needs of others near and far. As such, it is an opportunity to explore holiday traditions near and far. You might want to precede the play by having students make some simple one- or two-sentence presentations about the origins of traditions, stories, and legends that are commonly heard and experienced at the Christmas season. Have the presentations close with one in which a child tells how the original *Christmas Carol*, on which this play is based, was written in the 1800s by Charles Dickens in England. Others could talk about some of the following: the legends underlying the first Christmas tree in Germany; the Italian legend of Befana, the gift-giver; St.

Lucia Day in Sweden; Las Posadas parades in Mexico; and the luminaria tradition of the American Southwest. An all-in-one resource for such presentations is *Holly, Reindeer and Colored Lights: The Story of the Christmas Symbols* by Edna Barth, published by Clarion (1971).

Don't forget to include in the discussions other winter holidays such as Hanukkah, the Jewish festival of light, and Kwanzaa, the African American harvest festival.

To prepare children for this play, tell them the plot line of Dickens's original *Christmas Carol* that inspired the play. Talk about the similarities and differences between Dickens's story and the story in this play. Read aloud some excerpts from the original, a copy of which is readily available in most libraries.

WRITE IT

Dickens's story is full of references to English holiday and family traditions from holiday game-playing to foods eaten and songs sung. Have children think about their own holiday traditions during the winter months. These can include Christmas holiday customs, Hanukkah traditions, and New Year celebrations. Have them write a description of their

favorite winter holiday tradition. Since the lighting of candles appears in winter holiday events across cultures, you might have them glue their writings to candle shapes cut out of construction paper to place on a bulletin board entitled "Our Winter Traditions Light Up the World."

EXPLORE IT

This play is a modern-day version of Charles Dickens's classic Christmas tale, *A Christmas Carol*. Since the original story provides some insights into English holiday traditions, use this play effort as a springboard for discussing the origins of holiday stories and customs commonly seen in the United States each holiday season. As an English-inspired holiday craft, have children make mistletoe balls. The easiest way is to cut red construction paper into 12" by 1" inch strips. Each child gets two or three strips to decorate with holiday designs of his or her choice. The strips are stapled into circles and a small sprig of mistletoe is taped to the top inside of the circles. The ball can be hung with a yarn hanger. As an introduction to an English holiday food, you could make mince turnovers with children using pre-made pie crust and mincemeat. Go easy on the mincemeat filling as it is a strong flavor for most children. Be sure to ask about food allergies before serving.

Other holiday traditions often seen in the United States, but adapted from traditions around the world, are: the Christmas tree from Germany (explore by making simple tree decorations); ginger cookie treats from St. Nicholas when he visits Holland (explore by having children bake and taste gingersnaps); and the piñata from Las Posadas parties in Mexico (explore by making paper bag piñatas covered with fringed tissue strips and filled with hard candies). See *Holly, Reindeer and Colored Lights* referred to in the "Perform It" section.

READ ABOUT IT

Dickens, Charles. *The Christmas Carol* (public domain book available in many editions). Read aloud entire text or excerpts depending upon your students' sophistication.

Jackson, Ellen. *The Winter Solstice*. Millbrook, 1994.

Silverstein, Shel. *The Giving Tree*. Harper & Row, 1964.

To help explore multicultural winter celebrations, including Christmas, consider:

Chaikin, Miriam. *Hanukkah*. Holiday House, 1990.

Ets, Marie Hall, and Aurora Labastida. *Nine Days to Christmas: A Story of Mexico*. The Viking Press, 1959.

Pinkney, Andrea Davis. *Seven Candles for Kwanzaa*. Dial Books, 1993.

Singer, Isaac Bashevis. *The Power of Light*. Farrar, Straus & Giroux, 1980. (Read aloud)

75

CELEBRATING PEACE AND FREEDOM

THEY FOUGHT FOR FREEDOM

A CHORAL SPEAKING PRESENTATION

PLAYERS
SPEAKERS 1–30

SCRIPT

This script is in a choral speaking presentation format. Children can be standing on risers or steps for this presentation or in a single line, so long as all children can be seen. No change of physical location is necessary unless you choose to use props such as posters.

Teacher's Notes Begin on Page 82

SPEAKER 1: Our country is founded upon basic principles.

SPEAKER 2: These principles are democracy, justice, and freedom.

SPEAKER 3: Democracy gives us the right to vote and help decide how our government is run.

SPEAKER 4: Justice is having fair laws . . .

SPEAKER 5: And treating all people fairly.

SPEAKER 6: Freedom is the right to think, speak, and read what we choose.

SPEAKER 7: Our rights are in the Constitution and Bill of Rights.

SPEAKER 8: But sometimes the Bill of Rights has needed special help from special people.

SPEAKER 9: These people had their eyes on the land and its people.

SPEAKER 10: They saw that sometimes people had trouble.

SPEAKER 11: They were not treated fairly.

SPEAKER 12: The special people wrote books . . .

SPEAKER 13: And talked to government leaders . . .

SPEAKER 14: And made speeches about the problems they saw.

BASIC PRINCIPLES: simple, important rules

GOVERNMENT: in the United States, an organization by which the people rule themselves

CONSTITUTION: a written document that tells the government what powers it has and the people what rights they have

BILL OF RIGHTS: first ten amendments (additions) to the Constitution

SPEAKER 15: They knew our country would be a better place if all people were treated fairly.

SPEAKER 16: Each of these special people had a dream.

SPEAKERS 17–25: *[Each of these speakers makes a brief statement about a current or historical civil rights activist and what that person fought for. Depending upon the forum or holiday for which you prepare this presentation, you might choose African American leaders (Martin Luther King, Jr., Day presentation), women leaders (Women's History Month presentation), or a combination of leaders from different ethnic backgrounds who worked on different issues such as children's rights.*

An example of an activist statement is the following: "Martin Luther King, Jr., was a leader of the civil rights movement in the 1950s and 1960s. He fought for equality and justice for African Americans and all people." Depending upon the age of your students, you may want to limit activist statements to one sentence. Each statement is followed by all speakers stating: "He/She had a dream."

Other activists you might choose to use are Rosa Parks, Dorothea Dix, Cesar Chavez, Jane Addams, Elizabeth Cady Stanton, Susan B. Anthony, and/or Medger Evers.]

SPEAKER 26: Each of these people had a dream . . .

SPEAKER 27: And worked to make that dream come true.

SPEAKER 28: That dream is the American dream . . .

SPEAKER 29: A dream that our country will be a place where all people are treated with respect and fairness.

SPEAKER 30: We will reach for that dream in the way we treat others every day.

SPEAKERS 1–30: We all have a dream and you can share our dream too.

The End

81

TEACHER'S NOTES

PERFORM IT

For this performance children look nice when all dressed in the standard black and white stage outfit. In the alternative, they could all wear their "best" clothes for the choral presentation.

To precede this performance, you might choose to have several students read excerpts of Martin Luther King, Jr.'s, famous I Have a Dream speech. It is readily available in many literary collections. Check with your local librarian to locate a copy to share with your students.

You might want to close this play presentation with an inspirational song. Possibilities are standards such as "America the Beautiful" or "My Country 'Tis of Thee" or folk songs such as "This Land Is Your Land" or "If I Had a Hammer."

WRITE IT

You can create a writing project that dovetails with a decorative wall display by creating a "Footsteps to Peace" banner. When children study the civil rights movement, they learn about peace marches and demonstrations, some of which were led by Dr. King. Have them think about what the world needs and what they can do each day to help make the world (and their community particularly) a more fair, peaceful, and just place in which to live. Each child writes his or her idea on a card or piece of paper. On construction paper, the child traces his or her foot and cuts out the shape. Then the child glues his or her card onto the foot shape and glues the foot onto the banner.

EXPLORE IT

Give each child two 9" by 12" sheets of construction paper, one in a bright color and one in black. The child fan folds the colored paper and draws a paper doll shape on it so that the arms are at the paper's midpoint. The child then cuts out the paper doll and cuts the dolls apart. Children then trade three of their dolls with others so that they end up with four different dolls to glue onto the black paper. This cooperative project results in art in which the children of the world are symbolically depicted side by side. An easier version of this project is to have children trace and cut four versions of their hands and trade them. The hands are traded for other colors and glued to the black paper in a design of the child's choice.

Alternatively, have children create a peace wall—again, using black and colored paper. First, the class brainstorms words that help bring us to a peaceful place. These words include: *kind, fair, thanks, care,* and *love.* Children write their words in big letters on the colored paper, cut them out, and glue each word on a separate piece of black paper. They then cut shapes from colored paper that symbolize peace to decorate the word picture. Such shapes include the peace symbol, dove, olive branch, and heart. Children glue a shape onto each piece of black paper and then hang these posters on a wall or bulletin board.

READ ABOUT IT

Adler, David A. *Martin Luther King, Jr.* Holiday House, 1986.

Aliki. *Feelings.* Greenwillow Books, 1984.

Spier, Peter. *People.* Doubleday & Co., 1980.

Udry, Janice. *Let's Be Enemies.* Harper & Row, 1973.

Zolotow, Charlotte. *The Hating Book.* Harper & Row, 1969.

THE SECRET

PLAYERS

NARRATOR

RULER

COURT JESTERS **1–2**

COURT ADVISOR

CRIER

GREEN PEOPLE **1–5**

PURPLE PEOPLE **1–5**

ORANGE PEOPLE **1–5**

BLUE PEOPLE **1–5**

RED PEOPLE **1–4**

Teacher's Notes
Begin on
Page 90

COURT JESTER: entertains king or queen, often by doing funny things

COURT ADVISER: gives advice to a ruler

CRIER: reads important information aloud to townspeople

SCRIPT

As the play opens, the RULER *is sitting mid-stage looking very worried. He/She is surrounded by the* COURT JESTERS *doing tricks and the* COURT ADVISOR. *They are trying to cheer up the* RULER. BLUE PERSON 1 *and* ORANGE PERSON 1 *are to the side of the stage. They pantomime arguing with each other. Several other small groups of* PEOPLE *(all colors) can also be near or below stage. They also pantomime arguing.*

NARRATOR: Once upon a time, there lived an unhappy ruler. He/She ruled over a great many people. They were different from each other in some ways, but not so different in others. Unfortunately, in those days the people could only see the ways in which they were different from each other. They fought all the time. Why?

(BLUE PERSON 1 *and* ORANGE PERSON 1 *stop their pantomime to face the audience and speak.*)

BLUE PERSON 1: Why? We fight with the Purple People because . . . *(pausing thoughtfully)* . . . they are not blue.

ORANGE PERSON 1: Why? We fight with the Green People because . . . *(pausing thoughtfully)* . . . they are not orange.

NARRATOR: And so it went until one day. . . .

RULER: Nothing helps. My people are turning mean and cruel. Listen to them fighting out there.

(At this moment the actors on stage stop and listen, and all the different players from the color groups start fighting and yelling at each other.)

COURT JESTER 1 *(shouting over the arguing):* I'll just close the window.

(The JESTER pantomimes going to the window and closing it, at which time the actors cease arguing and freeze.)

DRASTIC: severe

COURT JESTER 2: But closing the window won't help. It's time for drastic action.

COURT ADVISOR: Yes, ruler, I think it is time to try . . . *(pausing importantly and then saying with wonder)* . . . the secret on them.

RULER *(shaking head):* Yes. Yes. You are right. Have the crier make an announcement.

ANNOUNCEMENT: notice of important information

(RULER, JESTERS, and COURT ADVISOR exit and CRIER enters carrying a large scroll. PEOPLE (all colors) enter at this time and listen with interest.)

HEAR YE: listen, you all; or, listen, people

CRIER: Hear ye. Hear ye. Our ruler announces a great contest. Starting tomorrow, all you citizens may head to the great mountain to search for the most wonderful treasure on Earth.

PEOPLE *(excitedly speaking all at once about how happy they are):* This is great! How wonderful. We will surely find the treasure first.

NARRATOR: The next day the Blue, Green, Purple, Orange, and Red People prepared for the treasure hunt. Each group began the journey in its own way.

JOURNEY: trip

(A two-sided sign with an arrow on both sides is placed on stage or can be held by a student. Enter the BLUE PEOPLE.)

BLUE PERSON 2: Look! This sign points to the treasure. Let's turn it around.

BLUE PERSON 3: Yes, then the others will get lost and we will find the treasure first.

BLUE PERSON 4: But do you think that is fair?

BLUE PERSON 5: Don't be silly. This isn't about "fair." This is about winning.

(*A* BLUE PERSON *turns the sign to face the opposite direction.*)

BLUE PERSON 1: Now, let's get going.

(*Exit* BLUE PEOPLE *in the direction the arrow pointed before they changed the sign, and enter* GREEN PEOPLE.)

GREEN PERSON 1: Wait here. Let's put some obstacles in the road.

GREEN PERSON 2: Yes, that will slow the other groups down.

GREEN PERSON 3: Do you think we should do that? Is that how we would want to be treated?

GREEN PERSON 4 (*acting snippy, mimicking* GREEN PERSON 3): "Is that how we would want to be treated?" Give me a break. This is about winning the treasure.

GREEN PERSON 5: Yeah, the bigger the obstacle, the better.

(GREEN PEOPLE *put boxes or other obstacles in the road. Exit* GREEN PEOPLE *and* enter ORANGE PEOPLE.)

ORANGE PERSON 1: Boy, am I hungry!

ORANGE PERSON 2: I don't know if we will make it. We didn't bring enough food.

ORANGE PERSON 3: I'm just weak from hunger.

ORANGE PERSON 4: I can't go on. I have to stop here for a while.

(*Enter* PURPLE PEOPLE *eating lots of food and looking very strong.*)

OBSTACLE: something that makes an effort harder

HEAR YE! HEAR YE! A ROYAL CONTEST TO FIND THE MOST WONDERFUL TREASURE on EARTH!

87

PURPLE PERSON 1: Oh, brother. Look at you guys. You will never get to the treasure.

ORANGE PERSON 5: You seem to have plenty of food. Could you share a little with us?

PURPLE PERSON 2: Not on your life. Do you think we're stupid?

PURPLE PERSON 3: Yeah, if you get stuck here that's one less group we have to beat to win the contest.

PURPLE PERSON 4: We'd be nuts to help you out. You might beat us to the treasure.

PURPLE PERSON 5 (*pleased with self):* So long, weaklings. We'll bring the treasure back so you can look at it—longingly.
(PURPLE PEOPLE *laugh as they exit.* ORANGE PEOPLE *limp and stagger offstage. Enter* RED PEOPLE.)

RED PERSON 1: I know nobody is ahead of us. We'll get to the mountain first, and the treasure will be ours.

RED PERSON 2: How do you know? How can you be sure?

RED PERSON 3: We know we're first because we cheated. You don't think we'd leave winning the treasure to chance, do you?

RED PERSON 4: But that's not fair!

RED PERSON 2: Fair is taking care of yourself first and . . . the others? Who cares?
(*Exit* RED PEOPLE. *The stage is empty. The* COURT JESTERS *bring the secret on stage. It is a box with a poster on the front that reads:"Be kind. Treat others as you would like to be treated." On the back side it reads: "Peace." It is covered by a cloth. When the prop is in place with* COURT JESTERS *guarding it, the* PEOPLE *[all colors] begin to arrive. They can ad-lib arguing about who arrived first.)*

LONGINGLY: with a strong wish for something

CHANCE: luck—good or bad

RED PERSON 3: So what is the big secret anyway? What's the treasure? *(The* COURT JESTERS *lift the cloth to show the sign. Enter* RULER *and* COURT ADVISOR.)

PURPLE PERSON 4: What kind of secret is that? Do you call that a treasure?

GREEN PERSON 3: Yes, where is the treasure?

COURT ADVISOR: If you know the secret, you can make the treasure.

ORANGE PERSON 3: What is this? Riddle time? Just tell us. What's the treasure? (COURT JESTERS *turn over the sign. On the flip side the word "peace" is written in large letters.*)

RULER: Now the treasure is within your grasp. Go home and try to find it in your lives. *(The* PEOPLE *[all colors] begin to exit, but as they do, they start to change a little. They are walking slowly offstage while the following exchanges occur.)*

PEACE: when people get along together without fighting

PURPLE PERSON 2: I don't get it. *(To* ORANGE PERSON) Are you still hungry? Here's a bit of bread.

ORANGE PERSON 2: Thank you. Do you need a wrap to warm yourself?

GREEN PERSON 2 *(to* BLUE PERSON): Here, let me move this obstacle out of the way.

RED PERSON 4: I'll help you. I know the way back home.

NARRATOR: After that day, little by little, the Ruler's people began to change. They thought about the secret and what true treasure was. Ever so slowly, they made peace.

The End

89

TEACHER'S NOTES

PERFORM IT

Costuming can be done with no-sew tunics where necessary. The Ruler's tunic could be a royal color, such as royal blue or purple, trimmed with a strip of white fiberfill or quilt batting to look like fur. The Jester can wear a clown outfit or any brightly colored clothing with a silly hat. The different actor groups portraying colors can wear the colors of their group or appropriately colored no-sew tunics. The Court Advisor and Crier can wear standard stage black and white clothing embellished with a brightly colored scarf or sash. The Narrator can wear nice clothing or stage attire.

There are many appropriate songs that provide an inspirational finish to this play. Consider the examples given in the "Perform It" section under the play "They Fought for Freedom." In addition, consider one or more of these popular classics: "Everything Is Beautiful," "One Tin Soldier," "Imagine," "What the World Needs Now," and "Hymn for Freedom."

WRITE IT

Have children pair up for this writing activity. Using pieces of 9" by 12" paper, children fold the paper into fourths. Each child writes the partner's name in the middle of his or her paper. Then the child proceeds to interview the partner. Children prepare four questions to ask the partner to help get to know him or her better and write the answer to each question in a full sentence in one quarter of the paper. The child then illustrates that sentence. For example, if the question is, "What is your favorite food?" and the answer is "pizza," the interviewing child writes: "Pizza is [insert name]'s favorite food," or "[insert name] likes pizza," and then draws a slice of pizza. Then the children reverse positions, and the interviewee becomes the interviewer. By this exercise, children get to know each other a little better and begin to form new awareness of others and, hopefully, new bonds.

Interview questions include questions about favorites as well as some questions on getting along. Sample questions include: What is your favorite food/color/television show? What is your hobby? What is your favorite sport? How do you try to get along with people? What do you think is important in a friend?

90

EXPLORE IT

Have children do hand art on 18" by 12" sheets of white construction paper. Each child traces his or her hand onto the construction paper. The child then asks five or six other classmates to trace their hands onto his or her paper. Some of the hands should overlap. The overlapping hands look something like a hand puzzle. The child then colors in the hand shapes and parts of hands in different colors for an interesting, abstract effect.

READ ABOUT IT

Baer, Edith. *This Is the Way We Eat Our Lunch: A Book About Children Around the World.* Scholastic, 1995.

Bunting, Eve. *Terrible Things: An Allegory of the Holocaust.* The Jewish Publication Society, 1980.

Coerr, Eleanor. *Sadako.* G. P. Putnam's Sons, 1993. (Story of Japanese atomic bomb victim and her attempt to fold a thousand paper cranes)

Lawlor, Veronica, sel. *I Was Dreaming to Come to America: Memories from the Ellis Island Oral History Project.* Viking, 1995. (Read aloud)

Levine, Ellen. *I Hate English.* Scholastic, 1989.

CHAPTER FOUR

CELEBRATING AMERICA'S HERITAGE

THINK
TALL

PLAYERS

JOHNNY APPLESEED

PAUL BUNYAN

BLUE OX

MOSE THE FIREMAN

STORMALONG THE SAILOR

PECOS BILL

SLEWFOOT SUE

JOHN HENRY

CHILDREN 1–8

TEAM MEMBERS 1–8

BOOKS 1–6

Teacher's Notes Begin on Page 100

SCRIPT

As the play opens, CHILDREN 1–8 *are sitting in the library look-ing very dejected. For a backdrop, use a paper panel affixed to the back of the stage that shows bookshelves filled with books.*

CHILD 1: Everything seems so impossible.

CHILD 2: I know what you mean. There is so much homework, and I don't understand it.

CHILD 3: I have this big report due soon, and I don't know how to start.

CHILD 4: And I don't understand what we learned in *[insert subject of children's choice, such as math, spelling, or reading]* today. The teacher went too fast. It's just impossible.
(From the sides or back of stage, JOHNNY APPLESEED, PAUL BUN-YAN, BLUE OX, MOSE THE FIREMAN, STORMALONG THE SAILOR, PECOS BILL, SLEWFOOT SUE, *and* JOHN HENRY *enter. They all speak loudly and swagger. They should look bigger than life. All of them are chuckling at what the children have been saying.)*

PAUL BUNYAN: What's all this complaining about?
(Children look around and are surprised to see a full-dress lum-berjack, blue ox, fireman, sailor, and others.)

CHILD 5 *(a little frightened):* Who . . . who are you?

95

BLUE OX: Who are we? Why, this is Paul Bunyan, and I'm his Great Blue Ox. And this is the famous fireman of New York City, Mose, and his friend, the famous sailor of the seven seas, Stormalong.

JOHN HENRY: And this is Johnny Appleseed, Pecos Bill, and Slewfoot Sue, and I'm John Henry, the man who beat the steam drill in driving steel to build the railroad. Who are you?

CHILD 5 (somewhat timidly): I'm . . . I'm just a kid.

MOSE: Just a kid! Why a kid is a great thing to be! We're here because we heard a lot of complaining. What's the matter?

CHILD 6: Oh, everything seems just impossible in school these days. We don't understand the work.

CHILDREN 1–8: And the teacher goes too fast in [insert the same subject inserted in script above]!

CHILD 6: It's just impossible.

STORMALONG: Nothing's impossible and we're just the ones to prove it. You know our stories, don't you?
(CHILDREN look at each other and shrug.)

PAUL BUNYAN: You don't? Why, I'm the lumberjack who dragged my sharp-spiked peavey across the west to dig the Grand Canyon!

BLUE OX: And I'm his strong blue ox, who survived the Winter of the Blue Snow.

JOHNNY APPLESEED: And I'm Johnny Appleseed, who planted apple trees from coast to coast.

MOSE: And I'm the most famous firefighter in the history of the City of New York.

STEAM DRILL: drill operated by steam power and used to break rocks

DRIVING STEEL: hammering steel spikes

LUMBERJACK: person who cuts trees into logs

PEAVEY: a spiked tool used by lumberjacks to move logs

GRAND CANYON: largest canyon in the United States; Colorado River flows through it

STORMALONG: And I'm the most famous American sea captain of the biggest ship from any coast.

PECOS BILL: I'm Pecos Bill, the cowboy who tamed the American West.

SLEWFOOT SUE: And I'm Slewfoot Sue, the famous catfish-riding girl.

JOHN HENRY: And I'm John Henry, the man who nearly built the railroad by himself.

ALL TALL TALE CHARACTERS (together): We're legendary!

LEGENDARY: larger than life

CHILD 7: Well, then, that's why you think nothing is impossible, but we are just kids. Lots of stuff is impossible to us.
(Enter TEAM MEMBERS 1–8. They look dejected.)

TEAM MEMBERS 1–8 (ad-libbing at the same time, without enthusiasm): Hi. How are you? What's happening?

CHILD 8: You guys look unhappy. What happened?

TEAM MEMBER 1: We lost again. It's just impossible. We're terrible players.

TEAM MEMBER 2: The other team has all the luck and all the talent. I give up.

JOHN HENRY: Give up! You should never give up!

TEAM MEMBER 3: Say, what is this? Dress-up day at the library?

CHILD 8: No. This is like a miracle or something. These guys just came out of the books to talk to us.

TEAM MEMBERS 1–8 (doubtful): Really????

PECOS BILL: You all have a real attitude problem here.

MOSE: You need to hear the amazing stories of some people who were just regular kids.

TEAM MEMBER 4: Amazing stories are not about kids like us.

SLEWFOOT SUE: Yes, they are. These people were kids just like you, and they thought things were impossible sometimes.

STORMALONG: But even though things looked impossible sometimes, they kept at it one step at a time. They accomplished the impossible.

TEAM MEMBER 5: Yeah? Like who?

JOHNNY APPLESEED: Like, for instance, listen to the stories these books have to tell.
(Enter BOOKS *1–6. These books are students holding posters in front of them, as though the posters are book jackets for books about the famous people. You can choose your own famous and courageous Americans to include here. The script material for books 1-6 is exemplary only.)*

BOOK 1: I'm the story of Wilma Rudolph. She was a little girl who was crippled by polio. She learned how to walk again and became a runner. She won three gold medals in the 1960 Olympics.

BOOK 2: I'm the story of Abraham Lincoln. He grew up with less than one year of school learning. He lost his first campaign for elected office but was eventually elected President.

BOOK 3: I'm the story of Sally Ride. She grew up, worked hard, and became an astronaut. She was the first American woman to travel in space.

BOOK 4: I'm the story of Harriet Tubman. She was born a slave, but escaped. Despite great danger, she ran the underground railroad and helped many slaves escape to freedom.

BOOK 5: I'm the story of George Washington Carver. He was born a slave and grew up very interested in plants. He worked and worked and developed over 300 uses for the peanut plant.

POLIO: a disease that can cause loss of movement or death

OLYMPICS: international sports contest held every four years

ELECTED OFFICE: a government job voted in by the people

SLAVE: owned by another and not free to make own life choices

UNDERGROUND RAILROAD: group who helped slaves escape

FREEDOM: ability to make life choices for oneself

98

BOOK 6: I'm the story of _____ .
[Stories abound for people overcoming disability, poverty, and hardship to achieve great things. It is preferable to have your students make suggestions for subjects after talking with parents and friends. If you are having difficulty coming up with people, some other possibilities are Jesse Owens, Louis Armstrong, and Cesar Chavez.]

TEAM MEMBER 6: Wow! I've heard of some of those people. They did do amazing things.

TEAM MEMBER 7: And I guess it wasn't always easy for them either.

MOSE: So, have you learned anything today?

TEAM MEMBER 8: Yes, we learned that hard work can make the impossible possible.

CHILD 1: But more than that! I learned that not only are people amazing, but places can be amazing too.

CHILD 2: Yeah, this library is about the most amazing place I've ever been.

TEAM MEMBER 1: I'm going to come back tomorrow and sit in the sports section. I want to see if maybe I'll meet [insert name of children's choice] there.
(All the actors smile and shake heads.)

PAUL BUNYAN: Well, you never know, with positive thinking and hard work, the impossible can happen.

The End

POSITIVE THINKING
believing that everything will work out right

99

From *Take A Quick Bow!*, published by Good Year Books. Copyright © 1997 Pamela Marx.

TEACHER'S NOTES

PERFORM IT

To costume this play, have Children wear regular school clothes and Team Members wear white T-shirts and shorts of the same color. You can hang numbers on the team members' backs. Johnny Appleseed, Paul Bunyan, Pecos Bill, and Slewfoot Sue can wear denim pants and plaid shirts, with the western characters wearing vests and cowboy hats as available. The Blue Ox can simply wear all blue clothing. Mose can wear all red and a plastic fireman's hat. Stormalong can wear all white and a sailor hat or a Greek fisherman's hat and peasant clothes. John Henry can wear a white T-shirt and plain colored pants. The books can wear the standard black and white stage clothing and carry large posterboard-sized "book covers."

To expand play performance, have children introduce each of the tall tale characters before the play begins. People in the audience may not be familiar with all of them or may have forgotten the tall tale legends that make them famous. Perhaps the actor for that character could come on stage while several other children take turns reading or reciting the fictional facts about each character's tall tale fame. Precede or follow the play by singing some story songs of folk heroes, such as "Ballad of Davy Crockett."

As you prepare for the play, talk with the children about the tall tale characters and the legendary feats of super-human prowess for which they are famous. In tall tales, the characters are often not just tall, but taller than mountains. They don't just sneeze, they blow trees down. Nutshell information about the play's characters follows:

Johnny Appleseed—a man who wore a pot on his head and walked the wilderness planting apple seeds

Paul Bunyan—a lumberjack who was bigger than any other, and who dragged his peavey through the ground to make the Grand Canyon

Blue Ox—Bunyan's reliable, larger than life ox, Babe, who survived the winter of the blue snow

Pecos Bill—the wild cyclone-riding cowboy who fell in love with Slewfoot Sue

Slewfoot Sue—a catfish-riding girl of the West who stole Pecos Bill's heart

Mose the Fireman—the most famous, daring fireman in the grand old history of the city of New York

Stormalong—the American sailor who traveled the seven seas

John Henry—the railroad builder

100

WRITE IT

Older children may want to try their hands at writing a tall tale. If so, have them make up their own tall tale character and write a short story about him or her. Otherwise, you might have the children write "simile" poems about one of the play's characters or another tall tale character of their choosing. The simile poem format is as follows:

[insert character name] is as tall as a

_____ .

He/she is as big as a _____ .
He/she is as strong as a _____ .
He/she is as loud as a _____ .

Children can add other characteristics that may be appropriate to their characters. These could include: jump as high as a _____, run as fast as a _____, eat as much as a _____, and the like.

Example:

Paul Bunyan is as tall as a mountain.
He is as big as a canyon.
He is as strong as a train.
He is as loud as the thunder.

EXPLORE IT

Ask your students to work in groups to explore in more detail the story of a tall tale character through the creation of story quilts. Each group explores a different tall tale character. The children read the story or listen to it (as told by you, or heard from a tape or compact disc recording such as a Rabbit Ears recording).

Then children make a paper reading quilt, made up of six- to nine-inch squares, to reflect the key events and happenings of the story. If making multiple story quilts is too large an undertaking, choose one tall tale character to explore in detail and have pairs of children work together to draw and color a scene from the hero's legend. Combine them all in a fifteen- to sixteen- square quilt.

READ ABOUT IT

Aliki. *The Story of Johnny Appleseed.* Simon & Schuster, 1963.

Cohn, Amy, comp. *From Sea to Shining Sea: A Treasury of American Folklore and Folk Songs.* Scholastic, 1993.

Krull, Kathleen, coll. and arr. *Gonna Sing My Head Off!* Alfred A. Knopf, 1992.

Below are excellent retellings found in the Rabbit Ears cassette or compact disc series on American Heroes and Legends:

John Henry, told by Denzel Washington with music by B. B. King.

Mose the Fireman, told by Michael Keaton with music by Walter Becker and John Beasley.

Pecos Bill, told by Robin Williams with music by Ry Cooder.

Stormalong, told by John Candy with music by NRBQ.

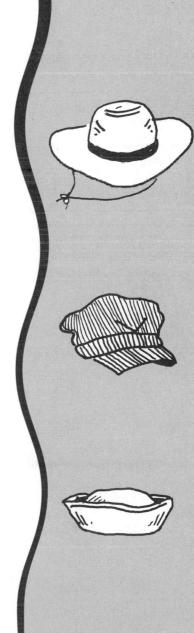

101

A COUNTRY OF GREATS

PLAYERS

CHILDREN **1–6**

GEORGE WASHINGTON

REVOLUTIONARY SOLDIERS **1–5**

ABIGAIL ADAMS

ABIGAIL'S FRIENDS **1–4**

JOHN ADAMS

PASSERBY

JOHN'S FRIENDS **1–2**

ABRAHAM LINCOLN

PRESIDENTIAL ADVISORS **1–3**

MARCHERS **1–3**

FARM WORKER ORGANIZERS **1-2 (OPTIONAL)**

Teacher's Notes Begin on Page 110

SCRIPT

Play begins with CHILDREN 1–6 *gathered around a box or an arch that will serve as the time machine. It can be a poster or mural affixed to the back of the stage that children pretend to get into. They can stand in front of it with their backs to the audience when they are time traveling.* CHILDREN 1–3 *made the time machine, and they are showing it to* CHILDREN 4–6.

CHILD 4: So you made this? This is great! (*Thoughtful pause*) What is it?

CHILD 1: What do you mean, what is it? It's a time machine, of course.

CHILD 5: Well, that's great. But why did you make it?

CHILD 2: We thought it would be a great way to celebrate *[insert name of national holiday you are celebrating—Presidents' Day, Memorial Day, Fourth of July, Flag Day]*.

CHILD 6: Wow, what a great way to find out firsthand what American history is really about! Does it work?

CHILD 3: We hope so. Get in and we'll try it.
(*While time machine is working [for about 5 or 10 seconds], you may want to turn lights off and turn on a tape of some mechanical or engine sound or ticking clock sound. When the sound stops and the lights go back on, the time travel has*

REVOLUTIONARY SOLDIERS: fought for the colonists during the war for freedom from England

ABIGAIL ADAMS: wife of John Adams and early voice for women's rights

JOHN ADAMS: second President; helped write the Constitution

PRESIDENTIAL ADVISORS: people who give advice to the President

MARCHERS: group who walks to protest unfairness

FARM WORKER ORGANIZER: helps crop pickers get better working conditions

TIME MACHINE: fanciful machine that can take people to the past or future

103

ended. Children turn and face the audience to signify they are out of the time machine.)

CHILD 1: Where are we? The dial says 1770s.
(*Enter* GEORGE WASHINGTON *and* REVOLUTIONARY SOLDIERS 1–5.)

CHILD 2: Look here come some people. Let's find out who they are. *(To the entering actors)* Who are you?

SOLDIER 1: We are soldiers with the Continental Army. We fight under General George Washington here (*points to* WASHINGTON).

SOLDIER 2: We are fighting the British.

CHILD 3: Why do you want to do that?

SOLDIER 3: The British are taxing us without asking what we think about it.

SOLDIER 4: They rule us from England. . . .

SOLDIER 5: But they do not know what we need or want.

GEORGE WASHINGTON: These brave soldiers are working for the freedom of our American colonies.

CHILD 4: Well, thank you for taking the time to talk to us about it.

CHILD 5: We know you have important work to do. Good-bye and good luck.
(GEORGE WASHINGTON *and* SOLDIERS *exit.*)

CHILD 6 *(excitedly):* That was interesting! Let's get in the time machine and go somewhere else in American history.
(CHILDREN *use whatever stage procedure you have agreed on to signify entry into and operation of the time machine.* CHILDREN *turn around to signify exit from the time machine.*)

CHILD 1: Where are we? The dial says 1780s.
(*Enter* ABIGAIL ADAMS *and* ABIGAIL'S FRIENDS.)

CHILD 2: Look, here come some people. Let's find out who they are.

CONTINENTAL ARMY: fought for the freedom of the colonies during the Revolutionary War

BRITISH: people from England, specifically, the king and government of England

TAXING: collecting money from people by government to pay for services

ENGLAND: an island nation in Europe; colonists came from there

FREEDOM: an ability to make one's own life choices

COLONIES: the thirteen British settlements that later became the United States of America

HISTORY: study of the past

104

Who are you?

ABIGAIL FRIEND 1: We are friends of Abigail Adams (*points to* ABIGAIL). This is Abigail. She is married to John Adams.

ABIGAIL FRIEND 2: John Adams is writing a constitution for the new United States, and we want to talk to him about it.

CHILD 3: Why do you want to do that?

ABIGAIL FRIEND 3: Because we have some important things to tell him. Here he comes now. Talk to him, Abigail.
(*Enter* JOHN ADAMS *and* JOHN'S FRIENDS.)

JOHN FRIEND 1: Abigail, John is just too busy today to talk to you. We arc writing the Constitution, you know.

JOHN FRIEND 2: There will be plenty of time to talk later.

ABIGAIL: Later will not do. John, when you write this new constitution, you must remember the women. You must give us more rights and treat us more fairly.

JOHN: Abigail, I know that is important, but writing the Constitution and getting agreement from all these people is very hard.

ABIGAIL: John, it's only the difficult things that are worthwhile. I will keep fighting for more rights for women.

ABIGAIL FRIEND 4 (*to* CHILDREN): Abigail works hard to get these men to think about women's rights. I wonder if they'll ever learn.

CHILD 4: Well, thank you for taking the time to talk to us about it.

CHILD 5: We know you have important work to do. Good-bye and good luck.
(*The* ADAMSES *and* FRIENDS *exit.*)

CHILD 6: That was interesting. Let's get in the time machine and go

> **CONSTITUTION:** a writing that tells the government what powers it has and the people what rights they have

105

somewhere else in American history.

(The CHILDREN *get into the time machine in the designated manner and, when they have completed time travel, they exit.)*

CHILD 1: Where are we? The dial says 1860s.

(Enter ABRAHAM LINCOLN *and* PRESIDENTIAL ADVISORS *1–3.)*

CHILD 2: Look, here come some people. Let's find out who they are. Who are you?

PRESIDENTIAL ADVISOR 1: This is President Abraham Lincoln, and we are his advisors.

PRESIDENTIAL ADVISOR 2: Mr. Lincoln is very worried. The country is torn apart by the Civil War. He knows that he must make an important speech soon.

CHILD 3: Why does he need to do that?

ABRAHAM LINCOLN: We still have slavery in this country, and something must be done about it. I must make a speech ending slavery.

PRESIDENTIAL ADVISOR 3: When the President makes that speech, some people will be angry, but he knows that it is the right thing to do.

CHILD 4: Well, thank you for taking the time to talk to us about it.

CHILD 5: We know you have important work to do. Good-bye and good luck.

(Exit LINCOLN *and his* ADVISORS.*)*

CHILD 6: That was interesting. Let's get in the time machine and go somewhere else in American history.

*(*CHILDREN *get into the time machine, time machine effects occur, and* CHILDREN *exit time machine.)*

CIVIL WAR: a war in the 1860s between the northern and southern states

SLAVERY: when people are owned by other people

106

CHILD 1: Where are we? The dial says 1960s.
(*Enter* CIVIL RIGHTS MARCHERS 1–3.)

CHILD 2: Look, here come some people. Let's find out who they are.
Who are you?

MARCHER 1: We are working with Dr. Martin Luther King, Jr. We
are marching for fair treatment for black people.

CHILD 3: Why do you need to do that?

MARCHER 2: Many people are treated unfairly. *[Optional: There are
laws that say black people must sit in the back of buses.
Some people are not allowed to vote.]* It is not right.

MARCHER 3: We know these things are wrong, so we are working
hard to change them.

CHILD 4: Well, thank you for taking the time to talk to us about it.

CHILD 5: We know you have important work to do. Good-bye
and good luck.
(MARCHERS *exit.*)

*[Optional Section: If you choose to delete this section
and want to provide additional students with speaking
lines, simply divide up lines for other play characters such
as the* REVOLUTIONARY SOLDIERS, PRESIDENTIAL ADVISORS, *and
the* ADAMSES' FRIENDS.*]*

CHILD 6: That was interesting. Let's get in the time machine and go
somewhere else in American history.
(CHILDREN *enter time machine, the time machine effects occur,
and* CHILDREN *exit from machine.*)

CHILD 1: Where are we? The dial says 1970s.
(*Enter* FARM WORKER ORGANIZERS.)

107

MIGRANT: moving from place to place

CHILD 2: Look, here come some people. Let's find out who they are. Who are you?

ORGANIZER 1: We are here to help the migrant farm workers.

CHILD 3: Why do you need to do that?

ORGANIZER 2: The farm workers work very hard in the fields, but they get very little money and live in very bad conditions.

ORGANIZER 1: It is wrong for people to be treated unfairly. We are here to help the workers get better working conditions.

CHILD 4: Well, thank you for taking the time to talk to us about it.

CHILD 5: You have important work to do. Good-bye and good luck.
(FARM WORKER ORGANIZERS *exit.*)

[End of Optional Section.]

CHILD 6: That was the best trip I've ever taken, but I think it's time to go home. Do we know how to get to *[insert current year]?*

CHILDREN 1–5: Let's try!
(CHILDREN *enter time machine, the effects occur, and then* CHILDREN *exit time machine.*)

CHILDREN 1–6: We're home!
(For a humorous touch, CHILDREN *can get down on ground and pretend to kiss the earth since they are so glad to be home. As they do this,* PASSERBY *enters.)*

PASSERBY: What's happening here?

CHILD 1: We just went time traveling through American history.

CHILD 2: We saw and met famous people.

PASSERBY: What did you learn?

CHILD 3: We learned that all through American history, there were great people.

CHILD 4: And do you know what made them great? They saw unfair things that needed to be changed, and they worked to change them.

CHILD 5: Sometimes it was dangerous or hard, but they didn't give up.

PASSERBY: That sounds like a really good history lesson.

CHILD 6: It's a lesson from history that we can learn from today. [*Optional:* With hope and hard work we can always change things for the better.]

The End

TEACHER'S NOTES

PERFORM IT

Children and Passerby can wear regular school clothing. Other costume ideas are premised on the children's use of white shirts and black pants (or dark skirts–long, if possible) and aprons (for girls playing colonial women). George Washington, Revolutionary Soldiers, John Adams, and John's Friends can wear vests with their outfits and blue, construction paper, three-corner hats. Abigail Adams and Abigail's Friends can wear white construction paper bonnets or skull caps with their clothing. Abraham Lincoln can wear a black, paper stovepipe hat with his costume. Marchers and Farm Worker Organizers can wear or carry signs that reflect their respective causes (e.g., "Equal Rights for All," "Join the Union," "Farm Workers Unite," and the like).

Children can sing any number of songs to precede and/or follow this play. These include:

"It's a Grand Old Flag"
"America the Beautiful"
"God Bless America"
"This Land Is Your Land"
"Yankee Doodle Dandy"

It also is very appropriate to precede the play by introducing the audience to some of the less familiar characters. You can do this by simply stating: "Today in our play you will be meeting some people from American history. Before we begin, we would like to tell you a little bit about them." Make sure the actors for these characters stand in front of the audience and bow as their "character facts" are being read or recited. Generally speaking, children as young as first grade are familiar with George Washington, Abraham Lincoln, and Martin Luther King, Jr. You will need to explain that John and Abigail Adams were Washington's contemporaries, that John was the second President of the United States, and that his wife, Abigail, was a strong advocate of women's rights long before the women's movement formalized. Abigail Adams's famous letter to John on women's issues is included in the Scott Foresman social studies series for grade 5. Introduce the farm worker issue by telling children about migrant farm worker leader Cesar Chavez, who worked in the 1960s and 1970s to organize laborers in California's Central Valley. The *World Book Encyclopedia* offers readily available reference information on any of these subjects.

WRITE IT

Have children write "our flag" poems using the format described here. This will provide an opportunity to talk about the different colors, stars, and stripes of the flag and allow for personal interpretation about what those parts of the flag mean to the children. Consider this as the format into which children plug in their ideas:

When our flag flies it looks _____.

Its blue [tells me to/reminds me of] ____.

Its red [tells me to/reminds me of] ____.

Its white [tells me to/reminds me of] ___.

Its stars [tell me to/remind me of] ____.

Its stripes [tell me to/remind me of] ____.

Example:

When our flag flies it looks like our history waving.

Its blue tells me to be strong and loyal.

Its red tells me to have courage.

Its white tells me to be fair with people.

Its stars tell me to reach high for my dreams.

Its stripes tell me to follow the lead of great people.

An easier writing activity for younger children is to cut out red, white, and blue shapes to glue onto black paper. On each color, children write words that the color reminds them of, keeping the flag theme in mind. Brainstorm some words for each color as a class before you begin and write them on the board.

Examples:

Red—brave, stripes, bright, bold

White—peace, star, stripe, pure

Blue—loyal, true, corner, sea

EXPLORE IT

As a creative way of exploring the features of the flag, have children make stars and stripes windsocks. To do this, cut 16" by 6" pieces of dark blue posterboard to form the cylinder at the top of the sock. Children cut out white stars to decorate this cylinder and glue them on, before you staple it into a circle. Then cut white and red crepe paper streamers 24" to 30" long. Staple or glue them in the inside of the cylinder and let them hang down. Hole punch the top of the cylinder on two sides and insert yarn for the hanger. You can use these to decorate your stage or auditorium area on the day of performance.

READ ABOUT IT

Adler, David. *A Picture Book of Abraham Lincoln.* Holiday House, 1989.

Franchere, Ruth. *Cesar Chavez.* Thomas Y. Crowell Company, 1970.

Parker, Margot. *What Is Martin Luther King, Jr., Day?* Childrens Press, 1990.

Young Abraham Lincoln. Troll Associates, 1992.

111

CELEBRATING DIVERSITY

THE MAGIC PEARS

AN ASIAN FOLKTALE

PLAYERS

FARMER, A GREEDY PERSON   TOWNSPEOPLE **1–19**

CHILDREN **1–3**   PEAR TREE

POOR WANDERERS **1–6**

Teacher's Notes Begin on Page 120

SCRIPT

As the play opens, FARMER *and* CHILDREN 1–3 *enter stage with wagon full of pears. The wagon can be any children's wagon. To illustrate pears, make a posterboard picture of a mound of pears. Support the picture with a triangular cardboard support on the back side of the picture. This pear prop can be easily removed from the wagon later in the play.*

CHILD 1: Oh, our pear tree gave us so much fruit this year.

CHILD 2: Yes, what a wonderful harvest it is!

CHILD 3: Think how much money we will make at market with these beautiful pears.

FARMER: Yes, children, we are very lucky. We will make lots of money with these pears.

(*The* POOR WANDERERS *enter and approach the* FARMER *and his/her* CHILDREN.)

POOR WANDERER 1: Oh, Farmer, you have so many beautiful pears, and we are so poor and hungry.

POOR WANDERER 2: May we have just one pear to share among us?

FARMER: How dare you beg from us? Go away.

CHILD 1: We must get to market with our pears. We worked hard for them.

POOR WANDERER 3: But you have so many.

HARVEST: the picking of grown fruits and vegetables

115

GREEDY: wanting more than one needs

POOR WANDERER 4: Surely you can spare just one.

CHILD 2 *(angrily):* Can't you hear? We said no!

CHILD 3 *(angrily):* Now go! Leave us at once.
(*During this time the* TOWNSPEOPLE *gather around and listen to the dispute.*)

TOWNSPERSON 1: I can't believe you, Farmer.

TOWNSPERSON 2: You are so greedy.

TOWNSPERSON 3: These poor people asked for only one pear.

TOWNSPERSON 4: How can you be so heartless and say "no" when you have so many?

FARMER: This is none of your business. Leave us alone.

TOWNSPERSON 5: Look, Farmer, can we buy a pear?

TOWNSPERSON 6 (*holding out money to* FARMER): Yes, here is some money in exchange for a pear.

TOWNSPERSON 7: That should please you, Farmer.
(*Money and pear exchange hands between* TOWNSPERSON 6 *and* FARMER. TOWNSPERSON 6 *gives pear to the* POOR WANDERERS.)

TOWNSPERSON 6 (*to the* WANDERERS): Here is a pear to share. Will that be enough?
(*The* WANDERERS *pantomime breaking the pear apart to share it with each other.*)

POOR WANDERER 5: Thank you so much. It is more than enough, because we have pears of our own. We want to share them with all of you.

TOWNSPERSON 8: How can that be? You said you were hungry and needed a pear.

116

From *Take A Quick Bow!*, published by Good Year Books. Copyright © 1997 Pamela Marx.

TOWNSPERSON 9: We don't understand. How can you share pears with us when you have no pears but the one you just received?

TOWNSPERSON 10: And, besides, if you have pears of your own, why didn't you just eat them?

TOWNSPERSON 11: Why did you ask the farmer for his pears?

POOR WANDERER 6: Well, we needed a few seeds. You will see. Watch.

(One of the WANDERERS *pulls out a hand shovel and pantomimes breaking up the earth. The others drop their seeds on this spot. The* TOWNSPEOPLE *crowd around this spot and the* FARMER *and his/her* CHILDREN *leave their cart and go watch the* WANDERERS. *Some of the* TOWNSPEOPLE *crowd in front of the* FARMER'S *cart and remove that part of the prop that shows the* FARMER'S *pears. As the* TOWNSPEOPLE *crowd around the* FARMER, *the actor playing the* PEAR TREE *gets into place where the* WANDERER *was hoeing. This actor crouches down in a ball.)*

TOWNSPERSON 12: Look, one of the pear seeds is growing.

(Actors clear area of stage in front of PEAR TREE.*)*

TOWNSPERSON 13: And so fast! It is a miracle.

(As TOWNSPEOPLE *speak,* PEAR TREE *stands and "grows" by spreading arms.)*

TOWNSPERSON 14: The tree is full of pears.

TOWNSPERSON 15: They are the biggest, most beautiful pears I've ever seen.

PEAR TREE: The pears of my branches grow many and sweet. There are no others like them.

TOWNSPERSON 16: How could the tree grow so fast?

MIRACLE: a wonderful happening that is impossible to explain

TOWNSPERSON 17: Those look like the tastiest pears ever.

TOWNSPERSON 18: It must be magic.

TOWNSPERSON 19: Wanderer, tell us how you worked your magic.

POOR WANDERER 1: Here. There are pears enough for all of you.
(Posterboard pears are taped with masking tape onto the PEAR
TREE*'s tree-crown prop [see "Perform It" section following
script].* WANDERER 2 *removes a few and passes them out.)*

POOR WANDERER 2: Take them. Take them until they are gone.
(TOWNSPEOPLE *begin to take the pears. They all pass them
around, share them, and pantomime eating the pears.
Children can ad-lib words of thanks and talk among themselves about how good the pears are.)*

TOWNSPERSON 1: Thank you so much, Wanderers.

TOWNSPERSON 2: The pears were wonderful.

TOWNSPERSON 5: You were so generous. Many thanks to you.

TOWNSPERSON 7: Now that the pears are gone, what will you do?

POOR WANDERER 3: What will we do? We will do this. . . .
(A WANDERER *proceeds to chop down tree with a cardboard ax.
As the* WANDERER *does this, the* TOWNSPEOPLE *gather around
the tree to cover its exit offstage.)*

TOWNSPERSON 1 *(pointing to the farmer's cart):* Look at the farmer's
cart.

TOWNSPERSON 16: It is completely empty. What happened to all the
pears?
(As everyone is looking at the cart, the WANDERERS *quickly and
quietly exit the stage.* FARMER *and* CHILDREN *gather around the
empty cart. They look very angry and ad-lib phrases such as*

"how did this happen," "this is terrible," "now we won't get any money at the market.")

CHILD 2: It was those Wanderers. They were thieves.

CHILD 3: Yes, they stole our pears. Where are those thieves?

TOWNSPEOPLE *(several speak here):* They are gone. The Wanderers are gone.

FARMER *(getting angry and stomping feet):* They can't be gone. They stole our pears! They stole our pears!

TOWNSPERSON 13 *(slowly, with meaning):* What does it all mean?

TOWNSPERSON 18: It means the greedy farmer and his/her greedy children learned a big lesson today.
(*All the* TOWNSPEOPLE *shake their heads "yes" and nod at one another and smile. The* FARMER *and* CHILDREN *look glum and shake heads "no" as they walk dejectedly offstage with their empty cart.*)

The End

TEACHER'S NOTES

PERFORM IT

The Poor Wanderers of this play can wear plain clothes such as white T-shirts and dark or beige pants; tie strips of ragged cloth around their heads and hang them over their shoulders. Using the black and white combination as the costume base, the Farmer, Children, and Townspeople can wear plain-colored, no-sew tunics belted at the waist in fabrics of dull earth colors. The pear tree can wear brown, or a brown no-sew tunic, and carry in front a tree-crown shape in green, cut out of posterboard onto which construction paper pears have been taped.

Since this play celebrates Chinese storytelling traditions, you might want to couple the play with reading or recitation by small student groups of nursery rhymes from China. For a useful reference book, see the "Read About It" section.

To ready children to perform this play, talk about the development of folktales and legends—how they begin as oral storytelling traditions designed to teach lessons and share cultural experiences. Talk about what lessons are taught in this play. Why might it have been told? Often, as with the story in this play, people tell stories to transmit positive community values—in this case, the concept of sharing and the evils of greed.

WRITE IT

A subject-related writing activity is to do a "four senses" poem using pears or other fruit as the subject matter. This poem is a four-lined poem that explores the subject as it relates to the senses of taste, feel, smell, and sight. The format is:

A pear looks like _____.
It feels like _____.
It smells like _____.
It tastes like _____.

Another writing activity is to have children write haiku from the Japanese writing tradition. See the "Write It" activity for the play, *Vivaldi and the Sound of Spring,* p. 23.

EXPLORE IT

You might want to make an easy classroom version of Chinese egg drop soup as part of the classroom play activities. To make the soup you need five to six cans of chicken broth, six diced green onions, and two eggs. Bring the broth to a boil in a soup pot. Have children break green onions into little pieces or cut them with plastic knives. Break the eggs into a small bowl and beat them with a fork to break up yolks and white. When broth is just under boiling, cook the egg with children taking turns. One child can stir the soup in a circular motion while another child holds a fork over the soup as a third student slowly drizzles the egg. The egg cooks as soon as it hits the broth. Add onions and serve immediately in polystyrene cups.

READ ABOUT IT

Wyndham, Robert, ed. *Chinese Mother Goose Rhymes.* Philomel Books, 1989.

Below are other Asian folktales you may wish to read to students to show them more about folk storytelling traditions:

Lee, Jeanne M. *Legend of the Milky Way.* Henry Holt, 1982.

Uchida, Yoshiko. *The Magic Purse.* Macmillan, 1993.

121

A TRICK FOR SLY RABBITS

A STORY BASED UPON AFRICAN STORYTELLING TRADITIONS

PLAYERS

NARRATORS 1–2	RABBITS 1–5
LION	BIRD
RHINOCEROS	DANCERS 1–5
HIPPOPOTAMUS	FISHERS 1–6
MOUSE	ANTS 1–2
GAZELLE	ANIMALS 1–3
GIRAFFE	

Teacher's Notes Begin on Page 130

SCRIPT

As the play opens, LION *is at center stage and* RHINOCEROS, HIPPOPOTAMUS, MOUSE, GAZELLE, *and* GIRAFFE *are nearby.* RABBITS 1–5 *are sitting at side of stage, lounging around.*

NARRATOR 1: On a day when the jungle was hot and the animals were thirsty, they all agreed they needed to dig a new well with fresh, clean water.

LION: Gather around, animals. We have a lot of work to do to dig this well.

(*Animals gather around* LION *to receive work instructions.* RABBITS *ignore* LION.)

MOUSE: We are ready to work, Lion. Big or small, we can all do our part.

(*Animals begin the work of digging and moving dirt. This can all be done through pantomime. The animals can even form a line and pass the dirt to each other using toy buckets or pails, as in an old-fashioned water bucket line for firefighting.*)

GIRAFFE (*looking toward* RABBITS): Rabbits! Why aren't you helping?

RABBIT 1 (*acting superior*): We're much too busy for such silly, unimportant work.

123

HIPPOPOTAMUS: Silly, unimportant work! How can you say that?

RHINOCEROS: Yes, we need water to live. What could be more important?

RABBIT 2: Pshaw! Do not bother us with such trivial things. Besides, we have to meet a friend.
(RABBITS *stand to leave and exit.*)

TRIVIAL: small and unimportant

NARRATOR 2: Finally, the animals finished their hard work. The new well was full of water—enough for everyone.
(*Animals leave stage area. Enter* BIRD *and* RABBITS *carrying berries.*)

BIRD: I'm glad we were able to gather all these berries. Should we eat a few?

RABBIT 3: Let's eat a few and then we will put the rest in a special hiding place so we can share them later.
(RABBITS 1–5 *and* BIRD *pantomime burial of the berries and exit,* BIRD *to one side and* RABBITS *to the other, waving good-bye to each other.* BIRD *leaves stage but* RABBITS *sneak back, dig up, and begin to eat the rest of the berries.*)

RABBIT 4: That silly bird. Now we can finish off the rest of the berries ourselves.
(RABBITS *eat all the berries and pat their tummies to show how full they are. Then one* RABBIT *has a sly plan.*)

NARRATOR 1: After the Rabbits ate all the berries, one of the Rabbits thought of a sly plan to trick Bird.

RABBIT 5: Bird! Bird!
(BIRD *reenters stage.*)

BIRD: Yes? What is it?

RABBIT 5: Look, Bird. All the berries are gone. You must have taken them, since you knew where they were.

BIRD: But, Rabbit, I did not take them. Really, I did not.

RABBIT 1: How are you going to pay us for them? Give us your biggest and best feather.

(BIRD *gives* RABBIT 1 *a feather and then leaves stage shaking his head.* RABBITS *laugh, whisper, and point at the outsmarted* BIRD. *Enter* DANCERS, *each holding ceremonial spears that can be made from wrapping paper rolls covered with colored papers and decorated with a few feathers or paper streamers.*)

RABBIT 2: Dancers, would you like this feather to decorate your spear or clothing?

DANCER 1: Yes, thank you.

DANCER 2: I will put it in my hair.

DANCER 3: Begin the drumbeat.

(*One* DANCER *begins beating a drum, which can simply be an old coffee can covered with construction paper.* DANCERS *form a circle and begin to take a few steps together. The* DANCER *wearing the feather removes it without drawing attention.*)

RABBIT 3: Hey, where is our feather?

(*All* DANCERS *look around.*)

DANCER 4: It's gone. The wind must have blown it away.

RABBIT 1: What! How are you going to pay us back?

DANCER 5: Here. Have this spear. You can spear fish with it.

> (RABBIT 4 *takes the spear and the* DANCERS *exit.* RABBITS *laugh and point at exiting* DANCERS. *Enter* FISHERS, *carrying pieces of net [the kind used for luau decoration].*)

FISHER 1: My net has a big hole in it.

FISHER 2: I am not quick enough to catch the fish with my hands.

RABBIT 4: Here, use this spear.

> (FISHER *takes the spear and spears a fish [made from construction paper with a circle of masking tape to which the spear will stick].*)

FISHER 3 (*to other* FISHERS): Here, take this fish to cook and eat.

> (FISHER 1 *takes fish and exits stage. Meanwhile,* FISHER 3 *drops spear. Other actors discreetly move it or kick it offstage.*)

FISHER 4 (*pointing):* Oh, no! Look! The spear is disappearing down the river.

> (FISHER 1 *reenters.*)

RABBIT 5: Where is our spear?

> (*The remaining* FISHERS *look around but cannot find it.*)

FISHER 5: It is lost in the river.

RABBIT 1: What? How are you going to pay us back?

> (FISHERS *look at each other.* FISHER 6 *pulls out a bag of grain and gives it to* RABBITS.)

FISHER 6: Here is a bag of grain.

> (FISHERS *exit.* ANTS *bring anthill prop onto stage. This can be a mound shape cut from a large piece of cardboard. The* ANTS *locate themselves behind anthill prop.* RABBITS *laugh and point at exiting* FISHERS *while this occurs.* RABBITS *start to walk once anthill is in place. The* RABBIT *carrying the bag of grain stumbles and drops the bag of grain down the anthill.*)

RABBIT 2: Anthill, you took our bag of grain. How are you going to pay us back?

> *(From behind the hill,* ANTS *enter.)*

ANT 1: You can take us, Rabbits.

ANT 2: The anthill sent us with thanks for the grain.

> (RABBITS *take the* ANTS *by the arms and walk with them offstage. Anthill is removed from stage. Enter* LION. *He sits guarding the well. Reenter* RABBITS *with* ANTS.)

RABBIT 3 *(to Lion):* We need some water. Give us some water.

LION: You did not help us dig the well, Rabbits. You cannot have water.

> (RABBITS *think for a minute.*)

RABBIT 4: Do you see what we have here, Lion?

LION: What do you have?

RABBIT 5: We have ants.

> (LION *thinks for a few seconds.*)

LION: I have an idea. You tie me up and give me the ants. Then you can drink.

NARRATOR 2: So the Rabbits tied Lion up very well and set the Ants down with him. Then the Rabbits went to the well and drank. When they were done drinking, they took baths so that the well water was all dirty.

(*As* NARRATOR *speaks,* RABBITS *go to the well and pantomime drinking and washing activities.*)

RABBIT 1 (*to* LION *in a teasing way):* Well, look at that! The well water is all dirty! Tooooo bad!

NARRATOR 1: And so the Rabbits left. But soon after the animals came to drink and found their water all dirty.

(*Enter* ANIMALS 1–3, RHINOCEROS, HIPPOPOTAMUS, GAZELLE, GIRAFFE, *and* MOUSE.)

MOUSE: Lion, you were supposed to guard the well. How did it get so dirty?

LION: It was the Rabbits. Look! They tied me up and tricked me into it by giving me these ants for a present.

RHINOCEROS: We will teach those Rabbits a lesson they will not forget.

GIRAFFE: The Rabbits just cannot do these things. Let's find them.

(*All the animals scurry about the stage and come back with* RABBITS.)

GAZELLE: Look what you did to our water, Rabbits.

RABBIT 2 *(looking):* So?

GAZELLE: It's dirty. It's no good for drinking.

RABBIT 2: So?

> *(All the animals gather together in a line and look menacing and angry.)*

ANIMAL 1: So, this! You can't trick us and ruin our water and get away with it anymore.

ANIMAL 2: You have to leave this part of the jungle.

RABBIT 3: We won't go. This is our home too.

ANIMAL 3: You will leave and you will leave now!

> *(The animals start walking all together toward* RABBITS—*perhaps in a menacing looking line.* RABBITS *start to look around, frightened all at once. Then they turn and run away.)*

NARRATOR 2: And so the animals chased the Rabbits out of their part of the jungle, and the Rabbits never came back. Everyone knows rabbits can be tricky and sly, but sometimes the Lion has a few tricks of his/her own.

The End

TEACHER'S NOTES

PERFORM IT

This play can be performed in conjunction with international days, Black History Month, or even as a springtime or environmental play, given the play's central use of the rabbits as characters and its emphasis on animal life.

To costume this play, have children wear no-sew tunics in colors appropriate to their animals, or have them carry large posterboard masks on sticks while wearing black and white stage clothing. The Dancers can wear earth-colored tunics decorated with a few feathers and perhaps feathers in their hair. They can also wear pipe cleaner armbands with crepe paper streamers. The Fishers can wear earth-toned tunics. Narrator(s) can wear nice clothing or the basic stage black and white clothing.

To expand performance of the play, children can close the play by singing one or more African folk songs. A resource for such songs is *Folk Songs from Africa* by Malcolm Floyd, published by Faber Music (1991). Other possible songs to close the performance with include "Circle of Life" or "Akuna Metata" from *The Lion King* soundtrack.

Finally, the performance of a folk dance from an African nation also provides a suitable segment for rounding out this play performance. Check your local library or school resource center for musical records or cassettes and appropriate dance instruction.

WRITE IT

An ideal writing activity in conjunction with this play is to have children write two-animal or tri-animal stories. These can be only a paragraph or can be the basis for longer stories. To do this writing project, the child picks two or three of the animals in the story and creates a new creature with characteristics of each of the original animals.

Example:

I am a girpottamus. I have a long neck and spotted, short fur. I reach high into the branches of trees to eat tender leaves. I have very short, thick legs that help me walk in mud and cool pools of water. I have a thick, wide back. When I am very tired, I curl my long neck and head onto my back for a nap.

EXPLORE IT

Cultures around the world, including those on the continent of Africa, celebrate festivals, religious ceremonies, and other community events using ceremonial masks. Often, these masks combine human and animal features. They are made with natural resources available in the region and can include grasses, wood, metal, shells, feathers, and seeds. Have children explore mask-making using heavy-duty paper plates. Cut human and/or animal facial features from construction paper and decorate with shells, feathers, foil, grasses, and seeds.

READ ABOUT IT

For African folktales that complement the play, consider:

Aardema, Verna. *Why Mosquitoes Buzz in People's Ears: A West African Tale.* Dial, 1975.

Haley, Gail. *A Story, A Story.* Atheneum, 1971. (Anansi spider story from the Ashanti people)

For cross-cultural rabbit tales, consider:

Han, Suzanne. *The Rabbit's Judgment.* Henry Holt, 1995 (Korean folktale)
Martin, Rafe. *Foolish Rabbit's Big Mistake.* Sandcastle, 1991. (Indian folktale)

131

CONDOR, BIRD RULER OF THE ANDES

A LEGEND OF THE SOUTH AMERICAN ANDES

CONDOR, BIRD RULER OF THE ANDES

PLAYERS

BIRDS 1–26

CONDOR

EAGLE

HAWK

SUN RULER

Teacher's Notes Begin on Page 138

CONDOR: a large and powerful bird of prey

SCRIPT

As the play begins, all actors except SUN RULER *are on stage. They sit or stand randomly as if in the midst of an important meeting.*

BIRD 1: I tell you, I'm tired of all this arguing and bickering.

BIRD 2: We never get anything decided. It's always complain, complain, complain.

BIRD 3: I know. Perhaps if we had a special ruler, he/she could resolve some of our disagreements.

BIRD 4: Yes, but since we never agree on anything, how will we agree on who should be our ruler?
(All the BIRDS *shake heads and nod.)*

BIRD 5 *(getting an idea):* I know. We could ask the great Sun Ruler. He/she can decide.

BIRD 6: I have an idea. All those birds who want to be our ruler can try to fly to the sun.

BIRD 7: That's a good idea. The sun is far away and only the strongest and bravest bird would make it.

BIRD 8: And if more than one bird makes it, the Sun Ruler can choose among them.

BIRD 9: Now, that is one great idea that we can all agree upon. Surely any bird who makes the long, hot flight to the sun will make a good ruler.

BIRD 10: When shall the contest begin?

BIRD 11 *(walking to one part of the stage and pointing):* Let all the birds who want to try to be our ruler gather here.
(BIRDS *12–14 and 24–26 remain in their places. All other* BIRDS, *including* HAWK, EAGLE, *and* CONDOR, *gather in the designated part of the stage to get ready for the flight. As a humorous touch have the birds strut, stretch, and do short jogs as runners do before a big race. As they do this, birds should try to look cocky and a little smug. The sun prop, which can be a fancy chair decorated in yellow, orange, and gold paper, is brought on the stage at a location far from the* BIRDS *or toward the back of the stage as space permits.)*

BIRD 12: All right. Are all you birds ready yet?

COMPETING BIRDS *(all nodding "yes" and ad-libbing these types of responses):* Yes, yes, yes. Let's go. We're ready. Let's do it now. Up, up and away.

BIRD 12: Okay. At the sound of the bell, the race will begin. The first bird to reach the sun will be our bird ruler.

BIRD 13: And if more than one of you arrives together, the Sun Ruler will decide who will rule us.

BIRD 14 *(ringing bell as he/she says "go"):* On your mark. Get set. Go.
[Alternatively, use a whistle instead of a bell and change the BIRD 12 *script line appropriately.]*
(The BIRDS *begin flying around the stage in a random way. After a few moments, several* BIRDS *start to tire and fall to the ground. When* BIRDS *"fall," they should go to the side of the stage and collapse there, looking very tired.)*

134

BIRD 15: Oh, I'm so small. I'm getting very tired.

BIRD 16: Me too. I guess I'm too weak to be ruler. I . . . I can't go on.

BIRD 17: I'm falling too. I . . . I can't do it. The sun is too far.
(BIRDS 15–17 *and* 1–3 *fall. The rest of the* BIRDS *continue to fly a bit longer. Then, they resume dialogue.*)

BIRD 18: Oh, I've tried and tried, but I can't make it.

BIRD 19: Me neither. But look, Eagle, Hawk, and Condor continue to soar.

BIRD 20: Well, I admit it. They are stronger than I am.

BIRD 21: And braver than I am. I'm out.
(BIRDS 18–21 *and* 5–6 *collapse to the side of main action.* EAGLE, HAWK, CONDOR, *and* BIRDS 22–23 *continue.*)

BIRD 22: Eagle, how do you keep going? I'm getting weaker and weaker.

EAGLE: I just fly. I beat my wings and soar.

BIRD 23: You, Hawk and Condor, you are stronger than me. I'm falling . . . falling.
(BIRDS 22–23 *and any others who are still flying collapse leaving only* EAGLE, HAWK, *and* CONDOR, *who continue flying.*)

HAWK: Condor, Eagle, only we three are left.
(*The three actors circle the stage in their soaring movement.*)

BIRD 24 *(pointing):* Look, only three birds are left.

BIRD 25: Yes, they are all the great strong birds—the Eagle, the Hawk, and the Condor.

135

BIRD 26: I wonder if they will all make it. The sun is still far away.
(BIRDS *continue flying movement for a few seconds before they begin to speak.*)

HAWK: Oh, no. I was sure I could make it, but I thought we would be to the sun by now.

EAGLE: It's getting hotter and hotter and still the sun is a long way off.

CONDOR: Do not talk. Just fly. Let the wind power your wings.

HAWK: I can't. I have no more strength. I can't make it.

EAGLE: The sun is too hot. I'm faint. I feel myself falling.
(EAGLE *and* HAWK *begin to falter and fall. As they sit, other birds come to help them while* CONDOR *reaches the sun.*)

CONDOR: I am here. I have reached the Sun Ruler's palace.
(SUN RULER *enters, coming to center stage.*)

SUN RULER: Condor, why do you come?

CONDOR: Sun Ruler, the birds of the Andes could not choose a leader. We decided that the bird who reached you could be leader, but I leave the final decision to you.

ANDES: large range of mountains in western South America that runs through Peru

SUN RULER: Condor, you are strong and brave. From the sun I rule the Earth, but you can help me. You shall rule all the birds of the Andes and your home shall be the highest mountain tops.

BIRDS *[all together begin cheering and clapping and simultaneously saying lines such as those listed below):* Yay! Hurrah for the new leader. The brave condor, our bird ruler. Hail to the condor! (CONDOR *leaves the sun and walks toward* BIRDS.]

BIRD 1: You have proven your bravery.

BIRD 2: You have proven your strength.

BIRD 3: You are worthy to be our ruler.

BIRDS *(all together):* Hail to Condor, Leader of us all, Ruler of the Highest Andes.

The End

WORTHY: to be of value and rightly honored

TEACHER'S NOTES

PERFORM IT

The Birds can wear no-sew tunics in bright colors. The Condor, Eagle, and Hawk can wear brown or black tunics, as appropriate. The Sun Ruler should wear all yellow with a gold paper crown. Wings can be cut from brown paper bags, but are not really necessary as children can pantomime flying with their arms held out.

This play offers subject matter suitable for international day events, multicultural celebrations, and Hispanic heritage events. It can also be used to complement basic world geography studies. Young children, however, have not yet studied much world-based curriculum. To enhance the meaning of the play to them in terms of its geographic and ethnic derivation, have them explore a little about South America and life in the Andes. Since the play is about birds, they might want to find out about birds of the Andes and perhaps other Andean animals such as llamas and vicuñas.

To expand the play performance, precede it with children's statements of some facts about the Andes. Such simple information might include: the countries through which the Andes run; the great ancient civilization of the Andes was the Incan Empire; Andean farmers grow food in the Andes using terraced farms; and some facts about indigenous birds and animals.

WRITE IT

Using birds and flying themes as the inspiration, let students try writing couplets. For younger children, writing a two-line rhyme is difficult enough. Older children may want to try to put four lines of poetry together. Be prepared for the struggle the children have with this project the first time you try it. If you do it several times, however, their competency increases amazingly.

To help children with the project, do some class brainstorming first. Write words on the board that have to do with birds and flying, such as: *fly, bird, wing, feather, beak, soar, high, low*. Then have children try to think of other words that rhyme with these words. They can write them on paper as you do so on the board. Armed with this preparation and a sample or two that you write on the board, they will begin to get the idea. For younger children, it is a worthwhile struggle. They are very proud of their completed poems.

138

Examples:

Birds can fly
In the sky.

A bird can sing
When on the wing.

Way up high
Condors fly.

EXPLORE IT

Since the play is about a contest involving flying great distances, consider doing some themed math measuring activities. The Andean birds find out who can fly the farthest. Have children make paper airplanes or straw flyers with paper fins, fly them, and then measure and record flown distances to see whose can go the farthest. This "math" activity combines components of aerodynamics with the measurement activity.

If you prefer a craft, use terra cotta–colored clay and let children create small Andean animals from the clay. They start with a fist-sized amount and pull an animal's features from the lump of clay. Children use toothpicks and pencils to make markings. These clay creatures are not unlike small statues, banks, and pots made and sold by adults and children in Venezuela and Peru.

READ ABOUT IT

Delacre, Lulu, sel. *Arroz Con Leche: Popular Songs and Rhymes from Latin America.* Scholastic, 1989.
McKissack, Patricia. *The Inca: A New True Book.* Childrens Press, 1985.

For other South American bird-themed legends, consider:

Flora. *Feathers Like a Rainbow: An Amazon Indian Tale.* Harper & Row, 1989.
Troughton, Joanna. *How the Birds Changed Their Feathers: A South American Indian Folktale.* Blackie, 1976.

139

TALE OF THE DUENDES

A STORY BASED UPON MEXICAN STORYTELLING TRADITIONS

TALE OF THE DUENDES

PLAYERS

NARRATOR

MOTHER

FATHER

GRANDMOTHER

CHILDREN 1–8

FRIENDS 1–8

DUENDES 1–10

Teacher's Notes Begin on Page 146

DUENDES: imaginary people who play tricks

SCRIPT

The stage is set with a table and two or three chairs. MOTHER, FATHER, CHILDREN, *and* GRANDMOTHER *are situated on the stage as though talking and playing games—perhaps after dinner activities.* GRANDMOTHER *should be seated. Brooms and dusters or cloths are located in two discrete places on stage.*

NARRATOR: Once upon a time there was a family. The family lived in a very nice house. They were proud of their house and always kept it very clean.

MOTHER: All right, children, it is time for us to clean up. No more games for now.

FATHER *(walking to the dusters and holding one out):* Here are the dusters and there are the brooms.

CHILD 1: We know how to do this, Father.

CHILD 2: We will clean every speck of flour and sugar.

CHILD 3: We will clean every crumb from our dinner.
(CHILDREN *sweep and dust for a few moments.*)

CHILD 4: Every spot is clean.

CHILD 5: Our job is done for today. It is time for sleep.

GRANDMOTHER: Yes, it is time for us all to go to bed. It has been a busy day, and you have worked hard.
(NARRATOR *speaks as family exits for bed.*)

NARRATOR: The mother, father, and children worked very hard to clean the house. No one went to bed until the house was in perfect order. Who would have thought that this could cause a problem? But that night. . . .
(*All the* DUENDES *sneak out from offstage areas and begin looking about. They are searching for something and seem to be puzzled.*)

DUENDE 1: I can't find anything.

DUENDE 2: Neither can I. Not a crumb or a scrap remains.

DUENDE 3: You would think such a fine family as ours could leave us just a little something to eat.

DUENDE 4: Yes, a crust of bread or a crumb of cake would be nice.

DUENDE 5: They are not very thoughtful.

DUENDE 6: No, they are not. How can we let them know that they are forgetting us?

DUENDE 7: I know. We can play a little trick.

DUENDE 8: Yes, then they will know we were here.

DUENDE 9: But what shall we do?
(*The* DUENDES *scratch their heads and think. They may whisper to each other and shake heads "yes" or "no."*)

DUENDE 10: I have an idea. Let's turn the chairs upside down. Then they will know we were here.

DUENDE 9: Then they will remember to think about us.
(*One or two* DUENDES *turn chairs over. Then the* DUENDES *sur-*

vey the scene, smile, and shake heads "yes" and sneak offstage. When they are gone, the family returns.)

CHILD 1: What happened here?

CHILD 2: Who did this?

CHILDREN 3–8 *(ad-libbing at the same time and shaking heads "no")*: I didn't. It wasn't me. Not me. (CHILDREN *can ad-lib their denials. About this time,* FRIENDS *1–4 enter stage as though dropping in for a visit.)*

FRIEND 1: What's the trouble, neighbor?

FRIEND 2: You look upset. Did something happen?

MOTHER: Look. The chairs are turned over.

CHILD 3: Who would do such a thing?

FRIEND 3: I don't know for sure, but I have heard of little people who sometimes live in houses with us.

FRIEND 4: We don't see them, but they are there. Some people call them "the duendes."

FATHER: "Duendes"? I have never heard of them.

NARRATOR: The family's friends left, and the family talked over what had happened. The family had a busy day and began their usual before-bedtime cleaning routine.

MOTHER: All right, children, it is time for us to clean up.

FATHER *(holding out a duster and pointing to the brooms)*: Here are the dusters and there are the brooms.

CHILD 2: We will clean every speck of flour and sugar.

CHILD 3: We will clean every crumb from our dinner.

ROUTINE: a usual and repeated way of doing things

143

(Family cleans for a few moments and fixes chairs.)

CHILD 4: Every spot is clean.

CHILD 5: Our job is done for today. It is time for sleep.

GRANDMOTHER: Yes, it is time for us all to go to bed. It has been a busy day, and you have worked hard.
(NARRATOR speaks as family exits for bed.)

NARRATOR: Once again, the house was in perfect order. Not a scrap or a crumb had been left behind.
(DUENDES sneak out from offstage areas again and begin searching for crumbs and scraps.)

DUENDE 1: I can't find anything.

DUENDE 2: Neither can I. Not a crumb or a scrap remains.

DUENDE 3: You would think such a fine family as ours could leave us just a little something to eat.

DUENDE 4: Yes, a crust of bread or a crumb of cake would be nice.

DUENDE 5: They are not very thoughtful.

DUENDE 6: No, they are not. How can we let them know that they are forgetting us?

DUENDE 7: Perhaps another trick is what we need.

DUENDE 8: Yes, with a second trick they will be sure not to forget us.

DUENDE 9: But what shall we do?
(DUENDES scratch their heads and think. They whisper to each other and shake heads.)

DUENDE 10: I have an idea. Let's take the chairs away this time and hide them.

DUENDE 9: Yes, then they will remember to think about us.
(Several DUENDES remove the chairs. Then the DUENDES sneak

offstage. When they are gone, the family returns.)

CHILD 1: What happened here?

CHILD 2: Who did this?

CHILDREN 3–8 *(refusing blame by ad-libbing these types of responses):*
I didn't do it. It wasn't me. Not me.
(FRIENDS 5–8 enter stage as though dropping in for a visit.)

FRIEND 5: What's the trouble, neighbor? What happened?

FATHER: Look. Our chairs are gone. Do you think it was the duendes?

FRIEND 6: Well, it might be. I have heard they do this kind of thing.

FRIEND 7: Do you know why they might want to trick you?

FRIEND 8: Do you leave anything out for them to snack on in the
evening while you sleep?

CHILD 5: No, we clean everything perfectly.

CHILD 6: Not even one crumb remains when we finish cleaning.

GRANDMOTHER: Perhaps that is the answer. Perhaps we can make
peace with our duendes.

CHILD 7: We can leave them a slice of cake each night.

CHILD 8: And a drink of cool water. Sharing with them should make for
a good peace.

NARRATOR: And that is exactly what the family did. Each night they left
out a treat or a snack, but they cleaned every other scrap
and crumb. The duendes were happy, and the
family was happy too.

The End

TEACHER'S NOTES

PERFORM IT

The Duendes should all dress in the same color and perhaps they can all wear simple, triangle-shaped hats. The family actors and Friends can wear regular clothing and ethnic Mexican clothing as available. If you prefer, instead of regular clothing, have children wear black and white stage clothing and accent it with paper flowers for girls' hair and brightly colored sashes for children of both genders.

Using the Spanish nursery rhyme book *Tortellitas Para Mama* by Margot C. Griego and others, published by Holt, Rinehart & Winston (1981), have children memorize and recite a few Spanish-language rhymes as an entertainment segment to precede the play. They should also be prepared to translate the rhymes for the audience. Mexican folk dances and songs can also be part of the performance. "La Raspa" and "El Pajarito" are both well-known and readily available folk dances for younger children. Possible songs include "Las Mañanitas," "De Colores," and "La Cucaracha."

"Little people" are part of the folklore of many countries. Some sources indicate that the *duendes* storytelling tradition may derive from European storytelling traditions originating in Ireland, Germany, and Scandinavia involving leprechauns, brownies, fairies, and gnomes. These story traditions may have been brought to the new world with the explorers and missionaries. These sources further reveal that the stories of little people have become part of the fabric of regional storytelling in different parts of Mexico. You can use this play with Cinco de Mayo celebrations, studies of life and culture of Mexico, and international or peace-themed events.

WRITE IT

In different parts of the world, "little people" from folklore look and dress in different ways. Have children think about the duendes, the little people of the play, and write a story or paragraph describing how they look and what they do. Children should indicate the kinds and colors of the clothes they wear, the work they do, their shape and size, and what they like to eat. Interesting versions of student-written duendes stories can be read to the audience before the play begins.

To make this writing activity easier for young children, have each draw a duende as he or she sees it. Then the child labels the duende's costume and writes a sentence or two stating the duende's name and one other fanciful fact, such as favorite food.

EXPLORE IT

This duendes play is based on regional Mexican storytelling traditions recorded in various sources. Explore another aspect of Mexican cultural life through art. Diego Rivera, Rufino Tamayo, and Frida Kahlo were famous Mexican artists. Children can create artwork in the style of any of these artists. Rivera is also probably the most famous muralist of his time. Many of his most famous works involve peasant people engaged in farming activities or with flowers such as lilies. The pictures are larger than life.

One effective way of having children explore Rivera's art is to use black construction paper on which they re-create part of a larger scene with pastels or colored chalk. Check the *World Book Encyclopedia* under the artist's name to locate a sample of the artist's work to show students.

READ ABOUT IT

Aardema, Verna. *Borreguita and the Coyote: A Tale from Ayutla, Mexico.* Alfred A. Knopf, 1991.

———. *The Riddle of the Drum: A Tale from Tizapán, Mexico.* Four Winds Press, 1979.

Mike, Jan M. *Opossum and the Great Firemaker: A Mexican Legend.* Troll Associates, 1993.

Yurchenco, Henrietta. *A Fiesta of Folk Songs from Spain and Latin America.* G. P. Putnam's Sons, 1967.

THE CHILDREN AND THE LEPRECHAUNS' GOLD

PLAYERS

NARRATORS 1–2   CHILDREN 1–10

LEPRECHAUNS 1–10   WANDERERS 1–8

Teacher's Notes Begin on Page 154

SCRIPT

When the play opens, LEPRECHAUNS *are situated in one part of the stage. They are engaged in a variety of activities, from making music with cardboard fiddle shapes, pipes, and drums to repairing shoes with small toy wood hammers.* CHILDREN *enter from different parts of the stage. At first they do not see the* LEPRECHAUNS. *As the* NARRATOR *begins to speak, there is the sound of Irish music and tapping in the background. Check your local library for cassettes of Irish music.*

LEPRECHAUN: a small, imaginary creature of Irish folklore

IRISH: relating to the country of Ireland

NARRATOR 1: One day a group of children went for a walk in the Irish countryside. Their families were poor farmers and the year's crops had not been good. They had little, but they shared what they had.

(CHILDREN *are walking when one stops suddenly to listen to something, and then the others stop to listen as well.*)

CHILD 1: I hear music.

CHILD 2: I hear tapping.

CHILD 3: No, no. I think it's music.

CHILD 4 (*pointing in the direction of the* LEPRECHAUNS): It's coming from over there.

CHILD 5: Let's go find out what it is.

CHILD 6 (*excitedly*): Go quietly, though. It may be leprechauns.

CHILD 7: If we can find them before they see us, perhaps we can make them give us their gold.

(CHILDREN *tiptoe quietly to area where* LEPRECHAUNS *are at work and play. As they tiptoe, the Irish music is louder. As* CHILDREN *near the spot where* LEPRECHAUNS *are, they speak.)*

CHILD 8: Look! There are the leprechauns. There are so many of them.

CHILD 9: Surely, this is our lucky day.

CHILD 10: But remember, once we see them we must never take our eyes off them. If we do, they will trick us, and we will lose them before they take us to the gold.
(CHILDREN *split up so that they surround* LEPRECHAUNS *before they speak.)*

CHILD 1: Aha! Leprechauns, you are captured.

CHILD 2: Don't blink or take your eyes off them.

CHILD 3: Leprechauns, you must take us to your pot of gold.

LEPRECHAUN 1 (*pretending to be afraid, perhaps winking at a fellow* LEPRECHAUN): I guess these children have us in their clutches after all.

LEPRECHAUN 2 (*dramatically, pretending overwhelming fear):* What shall we do?

LEPRECHAUN 3: We have no choice. We must take them to our gold.

CHILDREN 1–10 (*confident):* Yes. That's right. You must take us to the gold.

LEPRECHAUN 4 (*putting hand to ear as though hearing something in the distance):* We should start for the gold now. But wait! Children, I think I hear your parents calling for you.

CHILD 4: You cannot trick us that easily, Leprechaun. I still have my eyes on you all. Take us to the gold.

LEPRECHAUN 5: Yes, you are clever children. Well, we must be on our way.
(*Suddenly* LEPRECHAUN 5 *stops and cries out in fear.)*

CLUTCHES: held by someone or something

150

LEPRECHAUN 5 *(pointing):* But wait, children, look over there. There is a huge snake coming at us.

CHILD 6: You cannot trick us, Leprechaun. There are no snakes in Ireland. Take us to the gold.

(At this point, LEPRECHAUNS *1–10 shake heads, shrug shoulders, and start leading the* CHILDREN *around and off the stage to the sound of Irish music. Those* LEPRECHAUNS *with instrument props can pretend to play to the pre-recorded music you use.*

(While they are offstage on their walk to find the gold, two students unroll or uncover a large painted scene of clovers. LEPRECHAUNS *and* CHILDREN *break into two groups on their way to the gold. One group reenters and encounters* WANDERERS *1–4 as they enter the stage. The* WANDERERS *are tired, hungry, and poor.)*

WANDERER 1: Hello, children. How are you?

CHILD 7: You all look very tired and hungry.

WANDERER 2: Yes, we are tired and hungry.

WANDERER 3: We are farmers, but our crops did not do well this year.

WANDERER 4: We don't know what we shall do. The future looks bleak.

BLEAK: nearly hopeless

CHILD 8: You can come with us. We captured the leprechauns, and they are taking us to their gold.

WANDERER 1: Oh, how kind you children are!

WANDERER 2: Thank you for sharing with us. Will there be enough?

CHILD 9: Of course, there will be enough. Come with us.

(The other group of CHILDREN *and* LEPRECHAUNS *reenter stage and meet up at another spot on stage with* WANDERERS *5–8, who are also tired and hungry.)*

WANDERER 5: Hello, children. How are you?

CHILD 1: You all look very tired and hungry.

WANDERER 6: Yes, we are tired and hungry.

WANDERER 7: We are farmers, but our crops did not do well this year.

WANDERER 8: We don't know what we shall do. The future looks bleak.

CHILD 2: You can come with us. We captured the leprechauns, and they are taking us to their gold.

WANDERER 5: Oh, how kind you children are!

WANDERER 6: Thank you for sharing with us. Will there be enough?

CHILD 3: Of course, there will be enough. Come with us.
(*The* LEPRECHAUNS *of each group lead the* CHILDREN *and* WANDERERS *a few steps further so they reach the scenery of the field of clovers.*)

LEPRECHAUN 6: Well, here we are. The gold is here in this field.

CHILDREN *(in unison):* But where in this field?

WANDERER 1: The field goes on forever.

WANDERER 2: How can the children ever find the gold in there?

WANDERER 3: You leprechauns are trying to trick the children again.

LEPRECHAUN 7 *(pointing to a particular clover plant):* No, it is no trick. The gold is right there under that clover plant.

LEPRECHAUN 8: But you will need shovels to dig for it because it is very deep.

LEPRECHAUN 9: And you will need bags to carry it home because there is a lot of gold there.

WANDERER 4: Children, this is a trick. If you leave now, you will never be able to remember which clover plant the gold is under.

CHILDREN *(all say together):* What will we do?

CLOVER: a low-growing herb which has three-part leaves

WANDERER 5: I know. Have the leprechauns tie a red ribbon around the clover plant that has the gold buried under it.

WANDERER 6: Yes, that is a good idea.

> (WANDERER 7 *has a red paper ribbon with a circle of masking tape on back for this next part of the play. The red ribbon can be pressed onto the scenery to mark the special clover plant.)*

WANDERER 7 *(holding out a red paper ribbon):* Here is a ribbon that you can use.

LEPRECHAUN 10 *(taking ribbon and pressing it onto painted clover):* We can do that. I am tying the ribbon on now. The rest of you children and farmers must go get bags and shovels.

> (All the CHILDREN *and* WANDERERS *move offstage quickly except* CHILD 2, *who hides. While the others are gone, the* LEPRECHAUNS *get many more paper red ribbons and cover all the clover plants with red ribbons. When this is done, the* LEPRECHAUNS *leave, and the others return to the stage with bags and shovels or hand spades.)*

CHILDREN AND WANDERERS *(in unison):* Oh, no! The leprechauns outsmarted us after all.

CHILD 3: We cannot dig up the whole hill. We are lost.

CHILD 2 *(coming out of hiding):* No, we aren't. I stayed behind and marked the special clover plant. It is this one. *(Pointing to the first plant on which a ribbon was placed)* Dig here.

> (CHILDREN *pantomime digging and finding gold and passing it around to share with all.)*

NARRATOR 2: And that is how the children of Ireland outsmarted the leprechauns after all.

The End

OUTSMARTED: to think ahead and get what you want from someone or something

IRELAND: an island nation in Europe located next to England

TEACHER'S NOTES

PERFORM IT

It is fun to costume this play in shades of green. Have Leprechauns wear all green (or green, no-sew tunics) with green, felt, triangle-shaped hats. Children and Wanderers can wear the black and white basic stage clothing with green accents, such as green shawls, sashes, paper vests, and the like.

As a play extender, consider having children read or recite limericks. The origins of the limerick poetry form are unclear, but the witty, short poems are named after the city of Limerick in Ireland.

A fun song with which to close the program (since this play is about friendship, giving, and gold) is the traditional round "Make New Friends But Keep the Old." If children can learn to sing it as a round, it is lovely, but it also can be performed nicely if you break your singers into two groups and have one group sing one line, the next group the other, and so on, closing the song by repeating the whole round with everyone.

This play can be used in conjunction with St. Patrick's Day, international events, and multicultural celebrations. Prepare children for the play by telling them a little about Ireland, the "Emerald Isle." It is an island nation divided into two parts, about five-sixths Republic of Ireland and one-sixth Northern Ireland. Northern Ireland is allied with Great Britain, whereas the Republic of Ireland is independent. The country's official name is Ireland, but is often called the Republic of Ireland to distinguish it from Northern Ireland. The capital and largest city of Ireland is Dublin.

Ireland's folklore includes many stories about leprechauns. St. Patrick, for whom the holiday is named, is a well-known Catholic saint who is, by legend, credited with driving all snakes out of Ireland.

WRITE IT

A simple poem activity for children is to have them engage in a pre-alliterative exercise with the following poetry format. All the blanks in the format need to be filled in with words starting with the same letter (a letter of the child's choice), or, if the child is more advanced, adjectives and a noun, all of which start with the same letter.

154

This is a possible format:

My leprechaun's name is _____.

He/she works hard everyday to make ___.

He/she always wears a _____.

He/she likes to travel to _____.

He/she always brings me a _____.

Example:

My leprechaun's name is Sean.

He works hard everyday to make [shiny] shoes.

He always wears a [shimmery] shawl.

He likes to travel to Sweden.

He always brings me socks.

You can modify this poetry format to add any other fill-in sentences you like.

EXPLORE IT

Children love to make and eat candy peanut butter potatoes. It is a good measuring and cooking activity and always a successful treat. To make enough "dough" to make two potatoes per child, you need:

Dough

2 cups smooth peanut butter

1/2 cup softened butter

1 tsp vanilla

2 cups powdered sugar

Coating

1 cup powdered sugar

2 tsp cinnamon

4 tbsps cocoa powder

Cream butter and peanut butter. Add vanilla and powdered sugar and mix in these ingredients until smooth. If too sticky to work with add more powdered sugar. Then make teaspoon-sized, potato-shaped candies. When these are done, roll them in powdered sugar mixed with cinnamon and cocoa powder. You may want to coat the candies twice. This is a fun cooking activity for St. Patrick's Day.

READ ABOUT IT

Balian, Lorna. *Leprechauns Never Lie.* Abingdon, 1980.

Calhoun, Mary. *The Hungry Leprechaun.* Morrow Junior Books, 1961.

Gibbons, Gail. *St. Patrick's Day.* Holiday House, 1994.

McDermott, Gerald. *Tim O'Toole and the Wee Folk.* Puffin Books, 1992.

Shute, Linda. *Clever Tom and the Leprechaun.* Scholastic, 1988.

NORTHERN IRELAND

REPUBLIC OF IRELAND DUBLIN

EMERALD ISLE

CHAPTER SIX

CELEBRATING THE EARTH AND ITS CREATURES

HOW THE ELEPHANT SEES IT

PLAYERS

ELEPHANTS **1–5**   ANTS **1–5**

MICE **1–5**   BATS **1–5**

SNAKES **1–5**   SPIDERS **1–5**

Teacher's Notes Begin on Page 166

SCRIPT

As the play begins, the ELEPHANTS *are sitting and standing around the stage feeling very sad. With them are the* MICE, *and they are talking together.*

[*Optional introduction can be read by teacher or a student:* People often misunderstand nature's creatures who live near them. The elephant, for example, is a large animal but eats only plants. It does not fight unless it is in danger. Sometimes when the elephant looks for food, it mistakes people's crops for wild grasses. This makes people angry. Other animals such as bats are thought of as pests too. Bats are very important to all of us wherever they live because they keep insect populations in control. Enjoy our play about the important role all creatures play in nature's web of life.]

ELEPHANT 1 *(with confusion and concern):* You know, we may be big, but we only eat plants. Why do people keep saying bad things about us? They say we step on their crops and ruin their houses.

ELEPHANT 2: We can't help it. Often they plant their crops where we live. We don't mean to step on their houses. On the other hand, when people come after us to get our tusks, they do mean to hurt us.

MOUSE 1: Look, Elephants, I hate to see you let these things get you down. People have never understood us animals.

CROPS: plants grown in a plot of ground

159

MOUSE 2: Yeah. They don't understand how we work together. They just don't see that we each have an important job to do no matter who we are.

MOUSE 3: They say that we mice eat their food and that we are pests, but we just do what we are supposed to do. *(Pause)* Just like you do.

ELEPHANT 3: I don't know how we could act any differently. Mostly we're pretty gentle unless someone tries to harm us.

MOUSE 4: Look, you are just doing what you were put on this Earth to do. And that's got to be a good thing, no matter what anybody says.

ELEPHANT 4: I guess so, but it is so hard when you keep hearing about how many problems you cause.

MOUSE 5: Well, cheer up. Meanwhile, we've got to go do what we were put on this Earth to do—gather food. See you later. (*Exit* MICE *and enter* SNAKES.)

SNAKES *(winding and slithering movements to stage position):* SSSSSSSSSSSSSSSSSSSSSSSSSSSSSSSSSS . . .

ELEPHANT 1 *(sadly):* Hello, Snakes.

SNAKE 1: SSSSSSSSSSSSS. What are you so sad about today, Elephants?

ELEPHANT 5: Oh, people don't understand us. They say we ruin their crops and step on their things—as though we do it on purpose.

ELEPHANT 4: Usually they are in our living space.

SNAKE 2: SSSSSSSSSSSSSSS. People are hard to please. Look at us. They say bad stuff about us all the time.

SNAKE 3: They say we are sssssslimy and cold and that we just want to bite them.

SNAKE 4: But look at us. We have beautiful sssssscales, and we only go after food when we're hungry. We are so important to the balance of things.

SNAKE 5: We don't eat people. We eat sssssmall animals. If we didn't, there would be too many small animals. We help keep everything in balance.

SNAKE 1: We perform a real sssssservice, but people still call us scary and slimy. You just can't please people.

ELEPHANT 3: No, I suppose not. Thanks for trying to cheer us up.

ELEPHANT 2: We'll see you later, Snakes.

(*Exit* SNAKES *and enter* ANTS.)

ANTS (*walking all together in line like an army*): Hup, 2, 3, 4, Hup, 2, 3, 4, Hup, 2, 3 . . .

ELEPHANT 1 (*sadly*): Hello, Ants.

ANT 1: What are you so sad about today, Elephants?

ELEPHANT 5: Oh, people don't understand us. They say we ruin their crops and step on their things—as though we do it on purpose.

ELEPHANT 4: Usually they are in our living space.

ANT 2: People are hard to please. Look at us. They say bad stuff about us all the time.

BALANCE: to be in a condition where there is not too much or too little of any animal or plant in a natural community

ANT 3: They say we are pests and that we sting them and ruin their food.

ANT 4: But look at us. We work hard cleaning up crumbs and waste. We are so important to the balance of things.

ANT 5: But do people think about any of that? No! They just call us pests and step on us. They forget how important we are.

ANT 1: So you just have to keep doing your job, no matter what. You just can't please people, you know.

ELEPHANT 3: No, I suppose not. Thanks for trying to cheer us up.

ELEPHANT 2: We'll see you later, Ants.

> *(Exit* ANTS *and enter* BATS. *One* BAT *has a whistle and blows it between flapping motions.)*

BATS *(entering together with a jerky, flapping motion):* Flap up, flap down. *(Blows whistle.)* Flap up, flap down. *(Blows whistle.)* Flap up, flap. . . .

ELEPHANT 1 *(sadly):* Hello, Bats.

BAT 1: What are you so sad about today, Elephants?

ELEPHANT 5: Oh, people don't understand us. They say we ruin their crops and step on their things—as though we do it on purpose.

ELEPHANT 4: Usually they are in our living space.

BAT 2: Oh, that. You can't let those complainers get you down. You are at the top of your food chain. You are just doing your job.

BAT 3: Yeah, people say bad stuff about us all the time. They say we're dirty, and we like to bite them and tangle their hair.

FOOD CHAIN: the situation in nature in which larger animals eat smaller animals

BAT 4: And they say we're scary. Worst of all, they don't appreciate the important job we do.

BAT 5: Yes. We work hard every night keeping the insect population in control. We eat and eat and eat. We are very helpful.

BAT 1: But do you think people appreciate us? No! There's no pleasing people.

ELEPHANT 4: No, I suppose not. Thanks for trying to cheer us up.

ELEPHANT 5: We'll see you later, Bats.

(*Exit* BATS *and enter* SPIDERS.)

SPIDERS (*walking carefully, as though moving long legs*): One leg, other leg, other leg, other leg, other leg, other leg, other leg, other. . . .

ELEPHANT 1 (*sadly*): Hello, Spiders.

SPIDER 1: What are you so sad about today, Elephants?

ELEPHANT 5: Oh, people don't understand us. They say we ruin their crops and step on their things—as though we do it on purpose.

ELEPHANT 4: Usually they are in our living space.

SPIDER 2: People are hard to please. Look at us. They say bad stuff about us all the time.

SPIDER 3: They say we are scary and venomous and lying in wait to bite them.

SPIDER 4: But look at us. We have long, graceful legs, and we spin beautiful webs to catch our food. We are so important to the

APPRECIATE: to be thankful

POPULATION: all the living things of one kind that live in the same area

VENOMOUS: poisonous

LYING IN WAIT: hiding and waiting— often waiting to attack

163

balance of things.

SPIDER 5: Yes, we catch all sorts of small pests in our webs. We help keep everything in balance.

SPIDER 1: You elephants are just doing your job too. You are big and strong and you eat only grasses and plants. There's no pleasing people.

ELEPHANT 4: No, I suppose not. Thank you for trying to cheer us up.

ELEPHANT 5: We'll see you later.

(*Exit* SPIDERS *and enter* MICE 1–5.)

MOUSE 1: Are you elephants feeling any better?

ELEPHANT 1: You know, I think I do. We all have our jobs to do. We all are important.

ELEPHANT 2: And just because people complain about us, doesn't mean there is anything wrong with us.

MOUSE 2: That's right. Those people just need more information to understand you better.

MOUSE 3: Yes, it's important for all creatures on Earth to remember that they have important jobs to do. We are all important to the balance of nature.

MOUSE 4: Even us, no matter what anyone says!

MOUSE 5: Even cockroaches!

ALL ELEPHANTS AND MICE (*except* MOUSE 5) *(with disgust):* Cockroaches!

ELEPHANT 1: Hmmmmm. We may all need to think some more on that one, but we would probably find that you are right after all.

MOUSE 1: Yes. No matter what creature you are, you are important to the balance of nature.

The End

TEACHER'S NOTES

PERFORM IT

When costuming for animal and insect parts, consider doing so by color. For example, Elephants wear gray, Mice wear brown, Ants wear red, and Bats and Spiders wear black. For Snakes, no-sew tunics of a shimmery, scaly-looking fabric work well. If children do not have the color clothing suggested, use no-sew tunics in the colors indicated. To complete the elephant look, have children wear posterboard headbands onto which gray paper trunks and ears are stapled. For Mice and Ants, use bands that have small, brown, round ears for mice and two red paper antennae for ants. Bats can wear bands with large bat ears and also scalloped, black cloth capes that are tied at their necks. Spiders can wear loose neckbands with eight black crepe paper streamers stapled onto each.

To prepare children for the specific issue of the threat posed to long-term species survival (in this case, elephant survival), talk with your class about the play's premise—that is, that this large and generally peaceful animal has only humans as its predator. As human populations in its habitat increase and attempt to farm, human and animal needs clash. Elephants inadvertently break fences and trample crops. This makes farmers very angry, as they are not wealthy and need their crops. Additionally, hunters still poach and kill elephants so that their tusks can be harvested for ivory, a luxury item that humans do not need. The threat to elephants is an example of the animal endangerment issues that exist around the globe. Either before or after the play, children can state facts such as these as a performance extender.

WRITE IT

Continue exploration of the importance and fragility of nature's balance by doing a "web of life" writing activity. Have children think of six to eight creatures or plants to place at points on a circle by writing their names and drawing small pictures. In the center of the circle, they can write the words *water, soil,* and *sun.* Then the child writes sentences to connect one creature or plant on the circle with another. The sentence is written between the two points on the circle. If the child cannot think of a point on the circle that is connected to a plant or creature, a connection can be made to the center words.

Example:

Rabbit   *Tree*
Flower   *Bee*
Snake   *Hawk*
Grass   *Bird*

Rabbit eats grass.
Bird lives in tree.
Bee needs flower nectar.
Hawk eats snake.

An alternative activity is to have children write a food chain spiral. Starting at the center of a paper they write about the food chain from the bottom to top in a spiral manner. An example of such a spiral sentence is: *Grass is eaten by grasshopper, which is eaten by bird, which is eaten by mountain cat.*

EXPLORE IT

Have children continue the web exploration by making food chains. These can be made with paper chains about four links long. You can also make chains by quartering 9" by 12" construction paper and linking the paper rectangles with paper clips. The child draws a picture of each creature on a separate piece of paper and writes on the paper a sentence about what the creature eats. Punch holes at the top and bottom and connect with paper clips.

Another activity is to use the play's character of the elephant to explore fact and fantasy. Children are often exposed to more fanciful elephants (e.g., Dumbo, Babar) than they are real elephants. Build a bulletin board around "Elephants: Fact or Fiction?" Have children bring in fiction and nonfiction books on elephants and write simple facts under "facts" and fiction statements under "fiction." See example below.

READ ABOUT IT

Dorros, Arthur. *Elephant Families.* HarperTrophy, 1994.

Lauber, Patricia. *Snakes Are Hunters.* HarperTrophy, 1988.

———. *Who Eats What? Food Chains and Food Webs.* Harper Trophy, 1995.

Gray, Libba Moore. *Small Green Snake.* Orchard Books, 1994.

Van Allsburg, Chris. *Two Bad Ants.* Houghton Mifflin, 1988.

WHAT WE CAN DO

"Today if you will make a Pact
To help the Earth by just one act
the world will be a cleaner Place
And it will wear a Happy Face"

PLAYERS

NARRATOR

PRINCIPAL

STUDENTS 1–8

CHILDREN 1–5

CONTEST WINNERS 1–5

JUDGES 1–2

ADVERTISERS 1–3

ANNOUNCER

AUDIENCE MEMBERS 1–4

Teacher's Notes
Begin on
Page 174

SCRIPT

STUDENTS 1–8 *are gathered around the stage discussing Earth Day, School Beautiful Week, or any other clean-up or environmental event you choose.*

NARRATOR: One day not so many years ago, at a school not so different from our own, some students sat around talking about how to celebrate *[insert event name, e.g., Earth Day, School Pride Day].*

STUDENT 1: *[Insert event name]* is coming. What should we do to celebrate?

STUDENT 2: We need to celebrate it some way.

STUDENT 3: How should we do that?

STUDENT 4 *(the know-it-all type):* I know. Let's have an essay contest. And I'll be the judge.

STUDENT 5: No. No essays. But how about having a poster contest?

STUDENT 6: That's a great idea. The posters will be due in a week, and the whole school can participate.

STUDENT 7: That's great. But we'd better check with the principal and make sure it's okay.

ESSAY: a written, informative paper

PARTICIPATE: take an active part

169

STUDENT 5: And then we have to advertise. I'll get some kids to make announcements to the students.

STUDENT 3: And I'll arrange for some judges to pick the winners.

STUDENT 8: Uh oh. We still have a problem. We need a theme for the contest.

STUDENTS 1–7 *(all together, as though the air has been taken out of them):* Ohhhhh.

THEME: a particular general subject to be explored

STUDENT 4: Let's think. I know we can come up with something.
(All STUDENTS *sit thinking. They might tap their heads and otherwise look like they are concentrating. After a few seconds,* STUDENT 1 *speaks.)*

STUDENT 1: I have it! Can we use a theme like, "What You Can Do"?
*(*STUDENTS *talk among themselves and shake heads "yes.")*

STUDENTS 1–8 *(ad-libbing, talking all at once):* Yes. That's it. Let's get to work.
(All STUDENTS *exit stage. The next part of play is a series of short scenes that shows the* STUDENTS *and* ADVERTISERS *busy at work organizing the contest.)*

NARRATOR: And so the students at that school set to work to make their contest happen. There was lots of work to do. . . .
(Enter STUDENTS 1–2 *and* PRINCIPAL. STUDENTS *look as though they are in the middle of describing their contest idea to the* PRINCIPAL.*)*

STUDENT 1: So what do you think about our idea, *[insert principal's name]?*

STUDENT 2: We think it will help children think about how to keep *[insert appropriate reference, e.g., the Earth/our school/our community]* clean.

170

PRINCIPAL: I think this is a wonderful idea. You have my permission to go ahead. And we'll have an awards assembly to announce the winners.

STUDENTS 1–2: Great! Thank you.

> (*These three actors walk offstage. Enter, from another direction,* ADVERTISERS 1–3. *As they enter,* CHILDREN 1–5 *enter also from another part of stage or from the audience area.*)

ADVERTISER 1: Announcing the "What You Can Do" Poster Contest! Posters must be in by next Friday for judging!

CHILD 1: Can we enter?

CHILD 2: What do we have to do?

ADVERTISER 2: The contest is open to everyone at the school.

ADVERTISER 3: To enter, just make a poster on the theme, "What You Can Do" for *[insert appropriate reference, e.g., the Earth/our school/our community]*.

CHILD 3: That sounds like fun. I'm going to enter.

CHILD 4: So am I. And I have a great idea for a poster.

CHILD 5: Me, too. I think my poster will be about *[child can insert his or her idea for what the poster might be about]*.

> (ADVERTISERS *and* CHILDREN *exit stage in same or different directions.*)

NARRATOR: Finally, the day to turn posters in arrived, and the children brought their posters to school and turned them in.

> (*Enter* CHILDREN *and* CONTEST WINNERS *bringing posters to* STUDENTS 1–3, *who are standing center stage to receive them.*)
>
> [CHILDREN *can ad-lib appropriate submission and receipt phrases such as: "Here's my poster," "I hope I win," and "thank you."*]
>
> (CHILDREN *and* CONTEST WINNERS *leave and* JUDGES *enter.*)

ASSEMBLY: a gathering of people for a program

171

STUDENT 2: Judges, here are the posters.

JUDGE 1: Well, they look like the children worked hard. This will be a tough job.

JUDGE 2: We'll do the best we can. We'll tell you the winners as soon as we know.
(JUDGES *exit, talking among themselves.*)

NARRATOR: Finally, the day of the *[insert appropriate reference, e.g., Earth Day/School Pride]* program arrived. The children waited eagerly to see who won the contest.
(*At this point, all actors enter stage and sit or stand randomly around in front of the announcer area. The* ANNOUNCER *is in the center of the stage.* CONTEST WINNERS *are at the side of stage with their posters, along with* PRINCIPAL.)

ANNOUNCER: And now the time has come to announce our *"What You Can Do"* poster contest winners. Our thanks to all those who worked so hard to organize the contest. (Pause for polite applause from actors.) The winners are *[insert names of five students who will be presenting posters]*.
(*Again, all actors applaud as* CONTEST WINNERS *come to center stage.* ANNOUNCER *steps to the side.*)

CONTEST WINNERS 1–5: [CONTEST WINNERS *come to center stage and hold up their posters, and each makes a statement explaining his or her poster. When* CONTEST WINNERS *finish, they step to the side of stage and* PRINCIPAL *steps forward.*]

PRINCIPAL: Thank you all for this contest. Would anyone else like to come up and tell us a few other ideas for what you can do for the environment?
(*Children in audience raise hands and* PRINCIPAL *points to* AUDIENCE MEMBERS 1–4 *who come up.*)

EAGERLY: with great hope and excitement

AUDIENCE MEMBERS 1–4: *[Each* AUDIENCE MEMBER *takes a turn making a statement or two about what he or she can do to help the environment at school and in the community. Children can make up their own statements or these can be brainstormed as a class activity.]*

AUDIENCE MEMBER 1: If each of us can do just one of these things, *[insert appropriate reference, e.g., the Earth/our school/our community]* will be a better place.

ALL ACTORS *(standing on stage):*

Today we will make a pact
To help our school with just one act
Our world will be a cleaner place
And we all will wear a happy face.

The End

Today we will make a pact
To help our school with just one act
Our world will be a cleaner place
And we all will wear a happy face.

ENVIRONMENT: a place or community and the total conditions that affect it

173

TEACHER'S NOTES

PERFORM IT

This play is easy to costume. Students, Children, Contest Winners, and Audience Members can all wear regular school clothing. The other actors may want to be a little more formally dressed, that is, like an adult dresses. The Narrator, Principal, Advertisers, and Announcer can wear appropriate fancy dress for his or her gender. The Judges might wear the standard stage black and white dress. This play can be enhanced by opening the performance with the students' statement/recitation of an environmental alphabet. As a writing/art activity, assign each child a letter of the alphabet. Double up on letters as necessary. Each child uses his or her letter for a word and sentence about the environment. Then the child creates a poster around the letter-based statement on half sheets of posterboard. If you use these with the play performance, they are small enough for children to present easily.

Example:

A is for Acid Rain. Acid rain kills trees.
B is for Bats. Bats eat insects.
C is for Clean Up. Clean up trash and litter.

This play performance also can be lengthened by singing one or two environmentally themed songs at the end of the play, such as "Don't Go Near the Water" or "This Land Is Your Land."

This play can be used in conjunction with environmental curriculum and Earth Day, School Beautification Day, and clean-up events. To prepare children, talk about how important each individual's acts are and that small acts by many people can lead to big differences in the environment. Brainstorm with students what they can do each day—for example, walk more, pick up litter, save water.

WRITE IT

In addition to the environmental alphabet idea described in "Perform It," you can have children write Earth slogans. Since many slogans will be action-based, they can write them on cut-out hand shapes and mount them on a banner entitled "Busy Hands for Our Earth." Have each child write five slogans and pick the best one to be mounted on the board.

Examples:

Think Green.
Earth Work Is Good Work.
Recycling Is Right.

EXPLORE IT

Have children work individually or in pairs to interview different school staff, custodians, kitchen staff, the principal, other teachers, and students to find out what everyone around campus is doing to help the school environmentally and the community overall. Develop a short question list through class discussion. Have children write out the questions and then interview their parties. They can write a paragraph summary of the interview results if you like. You might even want to present some of the information along with your play or as part of an "Earth News" class publication.

Sample Interview Questions:

What is your name?

What is your job/position/role at school?

What do you do to help the school environment?

What do you see others do to help the school environment?

What additional things can we do to help the school environment?

READ ABOUT IT

Burton, Virginia Lee. *The Little House.* Houghton Mifflin, 1942.

Leedy, Loreen. *The Great Trash Bash.* Holiday House, 1991.

Lowery, Linda, and Marybeth Lorbiecki. *Earthwise at School.* Carolrhoda, 1993.

Peet, Bill. *Wump World.* Houghton Mifflin, 1970.

Seuss. Dr. *The Lorax.* Random House, 1971.

Interview Questions

1 what is your name?

2. What is your job/position/ role at school?

3 What do you do to help the school environment?

4. What do you see others do to help the school environment?

5. What additional things can we do to help the school environment?

175

CHAPTER SEVEN

CELEBRATING ART AND LITERATURE

MR. SHAKESPEARE'S POETRY GARDEN

"...That which we call a rose,
By any other name would smell as sweet..."

PLAYERS

CHILDREN **1–6**

FLOWERS **1–9**

ROSES **1–4**

ADDITIONAL ROSES

DAISY **1**

ADDITIONAL DAISIES

VIOLET **1**

ADDITIONAL VIOLETS

DAFFODILS **1–4**

ADDITIONAL DAFFODILS

Teacher's Notes Begin on Page 182

SCRIPT

As the play opens, all the different groups of flowers are standing or sitting on stage, steps, or risers as your stage allows. CHILDREN *1–6 enter.*

CHILD 1: This is a wonderful garden. Look at all the beautiful flowers.

CHILD 2: Wouldn't it be wonderful if the flowers could talk like they do in *Alice in Wonderland?*

CHILD 3: Flowers only talk in books. This is real life.
(FLOWERS *snicker and laugh quietly. Then they all say next line loudly in unison.*)

ALL FLOWERS *(loudly in unison):* This is real life too.

CHILD 4: Who said that? What's going on here?

FLOWER 1: We said it. The flowers. This is a magic garden.

FLOWER 2: The flowers that bloom here are so beautiful that we inspired the greatest poets of history to write about us.

FLOWER 3: One of the most famous of all writers wrote about us.

CHILD 5: And who was that?

FLOWER 4: That was Mr. William Shakespeare.

FLOWER 5: Would you like to hear what we can do?

CHILD 6: Yes, please. We would love to.

INSPIRED: to give life to or influence the making of something

POETS: writers of poems, often short lines that rhyme

HISTORY: study of the past

179

FLOWER 6: Roses, would you like to go first?

ROSE 1: We'd be glad to.

ROSE 2: You may have heard these lines before.

ROSE 3: They remind us of our wonderful fragrance.

ALL ROSES *(in unison):*

> Oh, be some other name!
>
> What's in a name? That which we call a rose,
>
> By any other name would smell as sweet. . . .

ROSE 4: Mr. Shakespeare wrote those lines for his play *Romeo and Juliet.*

FLOWER 7: Would you like to hear another poem from Mr. Shakespeare?

CHILDREN 1–6 *(in unison):* Oh, yes!

FLOWER 8: Daisies, violets. Are you ready?

DAISY 1: We are ready.

ALL DAISIES AND VIOLETS *(in unison):*

> Daisies pied and violets blue,
>
> And lady-smocks of silver-white,
>
> And cuckoo-buds of yellow hue
>
> Do paint the meadows with delight. . . .

VIOLET 1: That poem was from another one of Mr. Shakespeare's plays called *Love's Labours Lost.*

DAFFODIL 1: Mr. Shakespeare wrote about other flowers too—like us daffodils.

DAFFODIL 2: In his play, *A Winter's Tale,* he wrote about our blooming in spring.

DAFFODIL 3: Yes, he said we bring the sweet time of the year.

DAFFODIL 4: This is how he said it.

FRAGRANCE:
a sweet, pleasant smell

PIED:
spotted with many colors

LADY-SMOCKS:
a kind of flower

CUCKOO-BUDS: a kind of flower

ALL DAFFODILS:
> When daffodils begin to peer . . .
> Then comes in the sweet o' the year. . . .

CHILD 1: Well, this has been the most amazing visit to a flower garden I have ever had.

CHILD 2: It's been wonderful. Do you know any other poems?
[In this next part of the play, actors will read or recite either other famous poems written for children about flowers or, preferably, poems the students have written themselves. The line which CHILD 3 *says below should reflect which category of poems will be used in the next section.]*

CHILD 3: Do you know any poems by children like us?/Do you know any poems written for children like us?

FLOWER 9: I think we do. Let's try a few. *[Insert here some recitations by small groups of flowers. Preferably the poems will be couplets, haiku, or other short poems the students write themselves. If your children are young, the poems recited here can be those written by class effort. In the alternative, you can use poems from children's poetry collections that were written for children. See the "Perform It" section on p. 182 for some examples.]*

CHILD 4: You know, those poems sounded like the poems we wrote/learned in class last week.

CHILD 5: Yes, they do. How do you flowers know our flower poems?
*(*FLOWERS *giggle and whisper.)*

CHILD 6: I guess you really are a magic garden.

FLOWERS *(in unison):* Yes, a magic garden of flowers and verse.

The End

PEER: to look out, often in a curious way

SWEET O' THE YEAR: season of spring

TEACHER'S NOTES

PERFORM IT

Since this play is about a fanciful garden in which Shakespeare's flowers speak, the Children actors look nicest if they are dressed in tea party–type clothing. Dress the flowers in solid colors (e.g., Roses in reds, Daisies in white) or they can wear the basic black and white stage clothing and carry posterboard flowers. Alternatively, for younger children cut large flowers out of posterboard with a face hole cut into the flower's center. The child holds the flower mask up to his or her face to create the garden scene. Flowers 1–9 can be any assortment of flowers.

The text toward the end of this play has the Flowers recite the students' flower-themed poems. If your students are too young for this to be feasible, consider having them memorize and recite some classic children's poems about flowers and use the alternate script text indicated. Some appropriate poems are those by Christina Rossetti ("What Is Pink?") and Robert Louis Stevenson (e.g., poems from *A Child's Garden of Verse*).

Prepare children for this play by telling them a little bit about William Shakespeare. He lived from about 1564 to 1616 and was England's most famous playwright and poet. Because he lived over four hundred years ago, the language he used seems a little strange to us. Explain the poetry excerpts in the play as follows:

Rose text: Juliet wants Romeo to have a last name other than that of her family's enemy so her family will accept him. That's why she asks if a rose wouldn't smell just as sweet if it were called something else.

Daisy/Violet text: These lines are from *Love's Labours Lost. Daisies pied* means daisies of more than one color.

Daffodil text: In this song of spring, Shakespeare celebrates the blooming of daffodils, which marks the coming of spring.

WRITE IT

If your children are advanced enough to produce simple poetry to include in the last part of the script text, use that poetry writing activity as your related writing activity. Instructions on haiku are found in the "Write It" section after *Vivaldi and the Sound of Spring*, p. 23. Couplets are another poetry possibility. Keep them simple.

Example:
A daisy is white.
It is so bright.

182

Raindrop showers
Bring us flowers.

For another even simpler writing/art exercise, have each child choose a favorite flower and draw it on paper so that the petals are large and surround the center. In the center, the student writes the name of the flower. On each petal, the child writes an adjective describing the flower. More advanced children can write adjective-noun combinations. This is a different way to introduce adjectives.

Example:

Rose surrounded by adjectives such as red, soft, sweet, velvety.

Rose surrounded by adjective-noun combinations such as red petals, round petals, yellow center, soft petals, sweet smell.

EXPLORE IT

Since the most famous talking flower garden is probably the one conceived by Lewis Carroll in the Alice books, read to children from the original Lewis Carroll *Through the Looking Glass and What Alice Found There,* Chapter II, "The Garden of Live Flowers."

An enjoyable way to expand your cross-curricular exploration of this play is to do a flower dissection with your class. Children as young as first grade can successfully dissect and mount a flower on 6" by 9" sheets of posterboard. The flowers that work especially well for this age are alstroemeria and azaleas. Using a standard encyclopedia as reference for flower parts, you can help children find the petals, stamens, anthers, stigma, and pistil. Children can glue parts to posterboard and label them. Discuss how pollen from the anthers is transferred to the stigma to fertilize the flower.

Alternatively, explore famous artists by having students do Georgia O'Keeffe-style watercolors in which the children learn about her famous flower series. Children paint watercolor flowers on 9" by 12" paper. Before painting, they first sketch the flower so large that its petals "fall off" the edge of the paper.

READ ABOUT IT

Burdett, Lois, and Christine Coburn. *Twelfth Night for Kids.* Black Moss Press, 1994. (See also other titles in this Shakespeare Can Be Fun! Series.)

Krull, Kathleen. *Lives of the Writers: Comedies, Tragedies (And What the Neighbors Thought).* Harcourt Brace and Company, 1994. (Read aloud section on Shakespeare)

McCaughrean, Geraldine. *Stories from Shakespeare.* Simon & Schuster, 1995.

Morley, Jacqueline. *Shakespeare's Theater.* Peter Bedrick Books, 1994.

Stanley, Diane, and Peter Vennema. *Bard of Avon: The Story of William Shakespeare.* William Morrow, 1992.

THE MAGIC PALETTE

PLAYERS

TEACHER

PAINTBRUSHES 1–2

RED PAINT

BLUE PAINT

YELLOW PAINT

ORANGE PAINT

GREEN PAINT

PURPLE PAINT

WHITE PAINT

BLACK PAINT

PALETTE

STUDENTS 1–18

Teacher's Notes Begin on Page 190

SCRIPT

As the play opens, the PAINTS, PAINTBRUSHES, *and* PALETTE *are center, back of stage. They freeze. On stage, on the floor near them for easy access, are three large posterboards, each painted differently. One is drip/splatter painted in the Jackson Pollock style, one is cubist in the Pablo Picasso/Georges Braque style, and one is painted with strong, twisted strokes in the Vincent Van Gogh style. Students with drawing paper and pencils are located randomly around them. They are sketching and talking quietly. Enter* TEACHER.

PALETTE: a board used by an artist to lay and mix paint colors

TEACHER: Now, Students, take out your brushes and paints. It's time to do our weekly art project.

STUDENT 1: I hate art! My picture is never as good as everyone else's.

STUDENT 2: I know what you mean. I see something in my head, but my picture never looks like what I see.

STUDENT 3: That's how I feel too. My picture is never quite right.

STUDENT 4: How can you say that? You are a really good artist.

STUDENT 5: Yeah, you're the best artist in our class.

STUDENT 3: Well, that doesn't mean that I like everything I do.

(The PAINTBRUSHES *have been listening as the* STUDENTS *speak. Now they "wake up" to give the* STUDENTS *a little advice and counsel.)*

PAINTBRUSH 1 *(clearing throat and speaking with authority):* I think you students are a bit confused.

*(*STUDENTS *look around, surprised.)*

PAINTBRUSH 2: Yes, there isn't just one kind of painting that is good.

PAINTBRUSH 1: Each person is an artist, and you each have your own style.

STUDENT 6: Yeah, and my style is bad.

RED PAINT: Why do you think your style is "bad"?

STUDENT 6: No matter how hard I try, my pictures are messy with spots all over them.

STUDENT 7: Mine too.

BLUE PAINT: Spots all over them, huh? You mean a little like this? *(*BLUE PAINT *goes behind a posterboard "canvas" held up by two other* PAINT ACTORS *and pretends to paint vigorously to the sound of some exciting excerpt of music.* BLUE PAINT *then turns the picture around, and it is a drip/splatter painting in the style of Jackson Pollock.)*

STUDENT 7: Wow, that's exactly how my pictures look.

YELLOW PAINT: Well, then, you are in good company because this painting is like the work of a famous twentieth century painter named Jackson Pollock.

STUDENTS 6–7: Wowwwwwww!!!

STUDENT 8: Well, that's fine for you guys, but my pictures look strange.

STUDENT 9: Mine too. My faces seem sort of square-ish and odd. They look a little like a math paper on shapes.

ORANGE PAINT (*thoughtfully, tapping chin*): Shapes, huh? Math, huh? Sounds like geometry to me. Let me try something.
(ORANGE PAINT *goes to posterboard canvas held up by two* PAINT *actors and begins to work furiously. When the canvas turns, a cubist-style painting is displayed.*)

GREEN PAINT: Does your artwork look anything like this?

STUDENT 8: Yes, that's right. Doesn't that look a little strange to you?

PURPLE PAINT: What looks strange to one person looks wonderful and exciting to another.

BLACK PAINT: Yes, a very famous artist named Pablo Picasso invented a style of painting like this. It is called cubism.

STUDENT 10: Someone got famous for painting faces that look like a math paper?

PALETTE: Some people thought they looked strange, but lots more people thought they looked exciting and interesting.

WHITE PAINT: Picasso was always trying different styles and methods.

BLUE PAINT (*importantly*): Yes, that's true. Of course, his best period was that well-known period called his "blue period." (*Pause*) [*Optional:* Ah, such a great period of art!]

GREEN PAINT (*acting superior, but with a joking tone*): Oh, brother. How you do go on!

BLUE PAINT: You're just green with envy. That's your problem.
(GREEN PAINT *crosses arms as if in a huff.*)

STUDENT 11: But, wait! What is a "blue period," anyway?

STUDENT 12: I learned about that in a book I have. In his "blue period," Picasso painted many pictures all in shades of blue.

GEOMETRY: math study involving measurements, shapes, angles, and lines

CUBISM: a type of art using cube and cone shapes to make the pictures

187

MONOTONOUS: boring repetition; without change

INSPIRED: to give life to or influence the making of something

OPINION: a person's viewpoint on something that is not a statement of fact

STUDENT 13: Now that's a style I can get into. I always seem to start painting with a color and use that same color all over the place in the picture.

STUDENT 14 *(acting superior):* Monotonous. That's what I call it.

BLUE PAINT *(dreamily):* Inspired. That's what I call it.

PALETTE: You see, Students, people always have different opinions about art. It doesn't mean it's good or it's bad. It's just different.

STUDENT 15: Well, none of this helps me. My artwork always looks rough and really bright and all twisted up.

RED PAINT: Rough, huh?

WHITE PAINT: Bright, huh?

YELLOW PAINT: And maybe all twisted up, huh?

PAINTBRUSH 1: Sounds like one of history's most famous painters.

PAINTBRUSH 2: Yep, that sounds just like the work of Vincent Van Gogh. [*Optional Lines:* He's probably one of the most famous artists who ever lived, but when he was alive nobody bought his paintings because they thought they were too strange.]

(PAINTBRUSH 2 *goes behind a posterboard canvas held up by two* PAINT *actors and works furiously to music. The work is turned around and is in the style of Van Gogh, with twisting strokes and strong colors.*)

STUDENT 16: My art looks a little like that too.

STUDENT 17: I guess I see what you're saying. Art can be many different things and look many different ways.

STUDENT 18: Yes, there are many different styles of art, and different people like different styles.

BLACK PAINT: Art is a way of expressing yourself—your feelings and ideas.

WHITE PAINT: Art is not about good or bad. It's about saying something with a paintbrush and a box of paints.

STUDENT 14: Well, I think we all have plenty to say.

TEACHER: That's certainly never been a problem before. Why don't you all say something with your paintbrushes right now?

STUDENT 15: In our own personal styles?

STUDENT 16: Not good or bad?

STUDENT 17: Not right or wrong?

TEACHER: No rights or wrongs, goods or bads. Each of you is an artist. You paint it in your own style.
(STUDENTS *cheer and begin painting.*)

The End

EXPRESSING: to let others know your feelings

TEACHER'S NOTES

PERFORM IT

Costuming this play can be easy and fun. Have the Student actors wear regular school clothes. The Teacher can wear a fancy dress outfit appropriate to the actor's gender. Each of the Paints dresses entirely in the color of his or her paint.

(To make this easy, find out who has appropriately colored clothing before assigning parts.) The Paintbrushes should wear solid-colored brown or beige clothes. Make brown posterboard brush tip shapes stapled onto headbands (perhaps tipped with color) for the "brush" headgear. The Palette can wear plain colored clothing and hold or hang from his or her neck a large posterboard palette with spots of paint on it.

To expand this play, you might precede it with short biographical statements about the artists mentioned in the play and follow it with presentations on other artists your students have studied. Good choices are Claude Monet (based upon his impressionist gardens), Henri Matisse (based upon his "Jazz" papercut series), Georges Seurat (based upon his pointillism style), and Georgia O'Keeffe (based upon her flower series).

Each presentation can include basic information about when the artist lived, where he/she was born, what he/she liked to paint, and the style in which he or she painted. This part of the presentation is enhanced if you can show the audience posters or slides of reproductions of the artists' actual work.

To prepare children for this play, give them basic information on the artists covered and their styles:

Jackson Pollock: Born in 1912, he was an American artist. He was famous for dripping paint on a canvas laid on the floor.

Pablo Picasso: Born in 1881 in Spain, he was one of the most influential artists of the twentieth century. Famous periods of artwork include cubism, "blue period," "rose period," and collage.

Vincent Van Gogh: Born in 1833, he was a Dutch painter of the post-impressionist period. He had an extremely distinctive style involving bold color usage and strong, often twisted brush strokes. He often painted scenes of peasants and the countryside.

WRITE IT

Picasso's "blue period" paintings often connote sadness to people. Perhaps your students would like to write "feelings" poems in conjunction with a "blue period" art project or just as a writing activity. To do this, the child chooses a feeling (e.g., sadness, excitement, happiness, contentment) and writes that word at the top of the paper. Below that word, the child writes a sentence that gives an example of when he or she has that feeling. Below that, the child writes three verbs/nouns (as you choose) that remind him of that feeling.

Example:

Excitement
I am excited by the end of school.
Swimming, skating, bike riding

EXPLORE IT

Have the children explore this play through one or more art projects related to the artists mentioned in the play. They can do Pollock-style art by using watercolors to drip color onto paper. Have them create this art while listening to an interesting selection of classical or jazz music. Students can do cubist-style work by drawing a still life that fills a 9" by 12" sheet of paper and coloring it with crayon. When completed, the picture is folded so that there are eight rectangular folds. The child unfolds the picture, cuts it apart on the fold lines, and reassembles it in a new way on a second sheet of 9" by 12" paper. Children can draw Van Gogh-style pictures with large crayons or pastels. First, the child sketches the scene

(e.g., a single tree or branch with leaves) in pencil. Then the child uses bold, twisted, and wavy lines of color to fill in the sketched outlines. Encourage children to fill the paper with color—all done with the same strong strokes.

READ ABOUT IT

Venezia, Mike. *Jackson Pollock*.
    Childrens Press, 1994.
————. *Picasso*. Childrens Press, 1988.
————. *Van Gogh*. Childrens Press,
    1988.

Other titles are also available in the Childrens Press *Getting to Know the World's Greatest Artists* series.

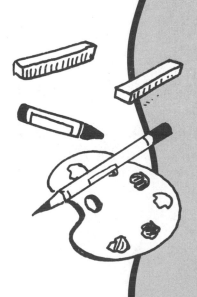

THE SCULPTURE GALLERY

PLAYERS

TEACHER	THE DANCER (NONSPEAKING)
TOUR CHIEF	RODIN INFORMATION STATION
TOUR GUIDES 1–3	DEGAS INFORMATION STATION
STUDENTS 1–20	NEVELSON INFORMATION STATION
THE THINKER (NONSPEAKING)	

Teacher's Notes Begin on Page 200

SCRIPT

As the play opens, STUDENTS *are milling about waiting for the start of a field trip. You might have one child hold up a sign that reads "Muscum Lobby."*

STUDENT 1: Borrrrring! Here we are on another field trip to a museum.

STUDENT 2: We only get one trip a year, and it's always to some museum with a lot of old stuff in it.

STUDENT 3: Yeah, and today we're going to look at statues. Statues are just a bunch of funny-shaped rocks. Like you said—borrrrring!

STUDENT 4 *(pointing to entering actors):* Look! Here comes the Teacher with the Tour Guides now.
(TEACHER, TOUR GUIDES 1–3, *and* TOUR CHIEF *enter.*)

TEACHER: Today we are going on a tour of the sculpture gallery. We will all meet back here later. Now, let's line up.
(STUDENTS *get into lines near their designated* TOUR GUIDES. *At this point, the* TOUR CHIEF *claps his or her hands to get everyone's attention.*)

TOUR CHIEF: I'm the head of the Tour Department. Welcome to our museum. I want to tell you about our wonderful new information stations.

SCULPTURE: three-dimensional art made from stone, wood, or other materials

GALLERY: a place that shows artworks to the public

TEACHER: Yes. At each sculpture you see, there will be an information station. To hear the information, just push the red button.

TOUR CHIEF: Enjoy your tours.
(*All actors leave stage. When stage is empty, the statue,* THE THINKER, *enters with the* RODIN INFORMATION STATION. *The* INFORMATION STATION *is a student who carries a sign that says "Rodin Information Station," under which is a six-inch red circle.* THE THINKER *goes to center stage and assumes the pose of the famous statue, and the* INFORMATION STATION *stands to one side. When these actors are in place,* TOUR GUIDE 1 *enters with* STUDENTS 1–7.)

TOUR GUIDE 1: All right, children, here we are at our first statue today. Who would like to push the red button?
(*Several* STUDENTS *raise hands and* TOUR GUIDE 1 *chooses one who walks up, pushes the button, and returns to place with other* STUDENTS. *In response to the* STUDENT *touching the red circle on the poster, the* RODIN INFORMATION STATION *begins to speak in a robotic or computerized sounding voice.*)

SCULPTOR: an artist who does sculptures

RODIN INFORMATION STATION (*sounding robotic*): This statue is called *The Thinker*. It was made by sculptor Auguste Rodin. Rodin was born in France in 1840.

TOUR GUIDE 1: Now, children, what do you suppose *The Thinker* is doing?

STUDENT 1 (*sounding bored*): Thinking, of course.

STUDENT 2: Of course he's thinking. The question is—(*pausing and really pondering*)—what is he thinking about?

STUDENT 3: You know, this could be more interesting than I thought it would be. What is he thinking about?

STUDENTS 4–7: *[Each* STUDENT *makes his or her own guess about what the statue model is thinking. Children can simply start their statements by saying: "I think* The Thinker *was thinking about. . . ."]*

STUDENT 5: Boy, this is fun, after all. It's like trying to find out a secret and only the statue knows the answer.

TOUR GUIDE 1: Well, you all did a great job. Now we must move on to the next part of the museum.
(TOUR GUIDE 1 *and* STUDENTS 1–7 *exit.* THE DANCER *and* DEGAS INFORMATION STATION *enter and take center stage.* DANCER *strikes a pose like an actual Degas statue. When they are in place,* TOUR GUIDE 2 *and* STUDENTS 8–14 *enter and place themselves around the statue so that it is still visible to the audience.)*

TOUR GUIDE 2: Who wants to push the red button?
(Several children raise hands and TOUR GUIDE 2 *picks one.* CHILD *walks up and pushes red button and returns to place with other children.)*

DEGAS INFORMATION STATION *(sounding robotic):* This statue is called *The Dancer.* It was made by Edgar Degas. Degas was born in France in 1834.

TOUR GUIDE 2: Now, what kind of dance do you think the dancer is doing?

STUDENT 8: Well, it's not hip hop.

HIP HOP: a dance with bouncy, sharp, gymnastic movements to fast, loud music

195

TWIST: a dance that involves twisting the waist and hips to the rhythm of rock 'n' roll music

STUDENT 9: And it's not the twist.

STUDENT 10: And it's definitely not the hokey pokey.

STUDENT 11: Oh, you guys. It's ballet, of course. But I wonder what ballet she is dancing.

STUDENTS 12–14: *[These children can make up their own lines about what ballet she might be dancing. For the children to do this effectively, they need to have heard parts of several ballets as part of class curriculum related to this play production. Sample statements might be:*

- *We studied Aaron Copland's* Billy the Kid *in school, but she doesn't look like she's doing a rodeo dance.*
- *And I've heard of Peter Tchaikovsky's* Swan Lake *but she doesn't look like a swan.*
- *Well, I think she's doing the "Dance of the Sugar Plum Fairy" and I'm getting hungry enough to eat a sugar plum right now—whatever that is.]*

SUGAR PLUM: a small, ball-shaped candy treat

TOUR GUIDE 2: Well, those are all good answers, but now it's time to move on.

(TOUR GUIDE 2 *and* STUDENTS 8–14 *exit.* THE DANCER *and* DEGAS INFORMATION STATION *exit. Enter* NEVELSON INFORMATION STATION *and students bring in boxes that make up Nevelson's sculpture [objects glued into boxes]. At this point,* TOUR GUIDE 3, TEACHER, *and* STUDENTS 15–20 *enter.)*

STUDENT 15: Wow, what is this? This is a lot different from the other sculptures we saw.

TOUR GUIDE 3: Who would like to push the button and find out more about this artwork?
(Several STUDENTS *raise hands, and* TOUR GUIDE 3 *chooses one. That* STUDENT *walks up, pushes red button, and returns to group of students.)*

NEVELSON INFORMATION STATION *(sounding robotic):* This sculpture is by Louise Nevelson. She created a series of artworks like these in which different objects were placed in box shapes. She was an American artist born in 1900.

STUDENT 16: But what is this sculpture about?

TEACHER: What do you think it is about? I don't have any magic answers. Tell me what you think.

STUDENTS 17–19: *[Students (who should have previously studied and discussed the "art-in-a-box" of Ms. Nevelson) can give their ideas about why Ms. Nevelson created these artworks, and what she was trying to say. They make their statements one after another.]*

STUDENT 20: Are any of those the right answer?

TOUR GUIDE 3: There really is no wrong answer. Art means different things to different people.

STUDENT 15: I like this. I wish there were really no wrong answers on tests at school.

STUDENT 20: These statues seem sort of like puzzles waiting to be solved by us.

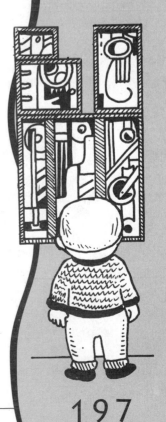

197

TOUR GUIDE 3: That's a great way to look at art—as a puzzle to be solved—but now it's time to return to your group.
(TOUR GUIDE 3 *and* STUDENTS 15–20 *exit, as well as* NEVELSON INFORMATION STATION. *The Nevelson sculpture is also removed. As tour groups with* GUIDES *and* TEACHER *reenter the stage, one student can hold up the "Museum Lobby" sign again.* TOUR CHIEF *enters stage from another direction at about the same time.*)

TOUR CHIEF: Well, children, what did you think of your tour?

STUDENT 16: It was much more interesting than I thought it would be.

STUDENT 12: It's really fun to look at a statue and try to figure out why the artist decided to make it.

STUDENT 14: It's a little like solving a mystery.

STUDENT 15: That's true. This field trip was pretty interesting, but there's something that remains a mystery to me.

TEACHER: What's that?

STUDENT 15: When are we going to lunch? I'm starving.

TEACHER: Where should we go?

STUDENTS 1–20: [STUDENTS *can insert a restaurant that is interesting and appropriate and then all shout it together while* TOUR GUIDES *and* TOUR CHIEF *shake their heads smiling or put hands over their ears. Examples of what can be called out are pizza or hamburger chains or local restaurants that are familiar and well-liked by children.*]

TEACHER (*sarcastically, shaking head and smiling*): Now, that's what I call culture.

CULTURE: art, music, and dance forms that are part of advanced community living

The End

199

TEACHER'S NOTES

PERFORM IT

This play can be simply costumed. Student actors simply wear regular school clothing. The Teacher should wear his or her own dress-up clothing. Tour Chief, Tour Guides, and all Information Stations should wear standard stage black and white clothing. The Tour Chief and Guides can wear large, official-looking paper badges. Information Stations can carry a large square of posterboard with a large, construction paper red circle and the words "Information Station" printed in black. The Thinker can wear all gray or plain-colored sweats to simulate the statue. The Dancer can wear traditional ballet clothing. The Nevelson sculpture is made from gluing objects into boxes, spray painting all boxes lightly in a single color (black or white), and stacking them on stage at the appropriate time. Photographs of Rodin's *The Thinker* can be found in *World Book Encyclopedia* and H. W. Janson's *History of Art* (1977). Nevelson's work can be found in the *World Book Encyclopedia* under both "Sculpture" and Ms. Nevelson's name. While you may not be able to find photographs of Degas's statues except in biographies of his life, his paintings of dancers are easily found under his name in the *World Book Encyclopedia*.

With respect to ideas for extending the play, consider preceding the play with some factual statements. These provide useful background information to an audience unfamiliar with the subject of the play. For this play, short biographical statements about Rodin, Degas, and Nevelson, as well as a general statement about what sculpture is (three-dimensional art), provide useful information. Have students divide into groups to research simple information about these artists, or provide students with several sentences of information for each sculptor (see text of play—script lines for Information Stations). Then have children take turns presenting the information to the audience.

Preparing children for this play involves not only introducing them to sculpture and the artists discussed in the play, but also letting children have the opportunity to listen to several ballets. Ideally, you can use this as an after lunch, "cool down and get quiet" activity. If you choose to use ballets for which suggestions are given in the play text, let children listen to Aaron Copland's *Billy the Kid*, Peter Tchaikovsky's *Swan Lake*, and Tchaikovsky's *The Nutcracker* (selected dances). Check with your local library to see if recordings are available for check out. These ballets are suggested because of their dramatic music and recognizable themes. Children generally respond well to them. *Billy the Kid* has familiar American and western sounds. Tchaikovsky's music is very dramatic.

WRITE IT

Ask students to write a biography poem about one of the sculptors discussed in the play or about sculptors of their choice. The poem can be written in an interesting manner, such as on a stair step or on the points of a star. The poem includes the name of the sculptor, a sentence about the kind of sculpture he or she did, the name of a particular famous artwork of the artist, three adjectives describing the artist's work, and a final sentence describing the artist's work critically.

Example:

Louise Nevelson
She made sculptures called "assemblages."
One was called "Sky Cathedral."
Black, modern, abstract
The sculpture looks strange.

EXPLORE IT

An obvious way to further explore sculpture is to let children work with clay. If you have no way to fire it, let it dry and have children paint it with a mixture of poster paint and white glue to give it some strength and stability.

Another way to explore sculpture is to have the children work in groups of about four students each to create a modern,

recycled art sculpture garden of their own. They could even invite the audience to visit the walk-through sculpture garden after the play. To make recycled art large enough to use in a walk-through area, have children bring in large cardboard boxes to glue and tape together to form their main structures. Then they can use clean, recyclable trash such as plastic bottles, cups, paper plates, newspaper, cans, and six-pack plastic holders to create the completed sculpture. The children should title the artwork when complete. Try to feel comfortable letting the children freely create. The art will look "strange," but it is the process of development and cooperation that is important.

Alternatively, let children use old egg carton bottoms to re-create Nevelson-style art. They glue found objects of all sorts into the carton spaces. When dry, spray paint the sculptures all white or all black as you choose.

READ ABOUT IT

Brown, Laurene Krasny, and Marc Brown. *Visiting the Art Museum.* E. P. Dutton, 1986.

Isaacson, Philip M. *A Short Walk Around the Pyramids and Through the World of Art.* Alfred A. Knopf, 1993.

Van Beek, Tom. *Degas, the Ballet and Me.* Checkerboard Press, 1993. (Read aloud)

CHAPTER EIGHT

CELEBRATING SCIENCE

PROVE YOUR HYPOTHESIS, PROFESSOR

PLAYERS

FAMOUS SCIENTISTS 1–6 *[Note: You and your students can decide upon which specific famous scientists of history to use. Some suggestions are Albert Einstein, George Washington Carver, Luther Burbank, Galileo, Isaac Newton, and Marie Curie.]*

STUDENTS 1–24

Teacher's Notes Begin on Page 208

SCRIPT

As the play opens, six SCIENTISTS *are at center stage discussing something among themselves. The children are seated in two groups on stairs or risers or, in the alternative, can enter and exit stage if there are no steps or risers. About half the children stand for each presentation. At the end, all are standing. The plot device is that the scientists of the ages are looking down at Earth. They are worried about whether anyone is interested in science anymore. As the scientists speak to each other, they can insert reference to each other's names. For example,* SCIENTIST 1 *below could say, "No, no, no, Professor Einstein," if you choose Einstein as one of your six scientists.*

SCIENTIST 1: No, no, no. It's very sad. Children just do not care about science these days.

SCIENTIST 2: It's true. They are too busy with sports and television and movies to think about science.

SCIENTIST 3: I'm not sure you are right. *[Insert scientist's name]* and I have been looking at Earth lately in our travels, and we think science is alive and well.

SCIENTIST 4: You think so? Then I suggest, *[insert name of scientist 3]*, that you prove your hypothesis.

HYPOTHESIS: an educated guess

205

SCIENTIST 5: We will. Let's see. Here comes a group of students now. Let's see what they think about science.
(STUDENTS 1–9 *and* STUDENTS 19–21 *either stand in their places or, if previously offstage, enter now.*)

SCIENTIST 1: Students, we are having a disagreement about whether children today are interested in science. Can you help us?

SCIENTIST 3: Yes, can you tell us what you have been learning about science, and if you like it?

STUDENT 1: Yes, this year we learned all about *[insert student-written statement of scientific subject].*

STUDENTS 2–4: [*These students present posters and say a line or two about what they learned in the subject stated by* STUDENT 1.]

SCIENTIST 4: Yes, that's very interesting, but it only proves that you had to study science in school.

STUDENT 5: But I was so interested, I checked out a library book and did some experiments at home.

STUDENT 6: And I went to our local museum to see a special exhibit.

STUDENT 7: I went to the bookstore and bought a book about the subject that interested me most.

STUDENT 8: We like studying science. You can get your hands dirty with experiments and all.

STUDENT 9: Yeah, it's as good as art class, where you can also get really messy.
(STUDENTS 1–9 *and* STUDENTS 19–21 *sit or exit as appropriate.*)

SCIENTIST 5: You see what we mean. Kids do like science.

SCIENTIST 4: Oh, I don't know. That's just one group of kids.

SCIENTIST 3: Well, here comes another group. Let's hear what they have to say.

(STUDENTS 10–18 and STUDENTS 22–24 stand or enter.)

SCIENTIST 6: Students, can you tell us something? We want to know if children today are interested in science.

STUDENT 10: Oh, yes. We were just talking about what we've been learning.

STUDENTS 11–18: [STUDENTS 11–18 *make their brief presentations on what they have been studying.*]

STUDENT 10: We thought what we learned was so interesting, we would go find out more at the library.

(STUDENTS 1–9 reenter together with STUDENTS 19–21.)

SCIENTIST 1: Well, thank you. You all have convinced me.

SCIENTISTS 2 AND 4 *(in unison)*: And us.

SCIENTIST 4: Children today are still interested in science.

SCIENTIST 6: What other scientific subjects do you children want to investigate?

(All students stand at this time if not already standing.)

STUDENT 19: I want to learn about *[inserts the subject he or she wants to learn more about].*

STUDENTS 20–24: [Take turns stating the scientific subjects they want to learn more about.]

SCIENTIST 1: Well, this is great! Science is alive and well for children on Earth.

STUDENT 20: Well, we can't say it about the whole Earth and all the kids on it, but. . . .

STUDENTS 1–24 *(all together)*: Science is alive and well at *[insert name of school].*

The End

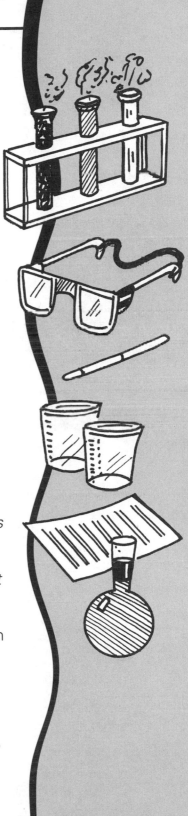

207

TEACHER'S NOTES

PERFORM IT

Since most of the actors play Students, costuming is quite easy. All Students wear regular school clothing. The Scientists should wear standard black and white stage clothing as the costume base. Add plain white aprons and jackets (that look like lab apparel), if possible; these, together with glasses without lenses and clipboards will give the proper scientist look. Since scientists are renowned for their eccentricities, children may want to augment these simple costumes with interesting Einstein-type wigs and the like.

For a play extender that is appropriate either before or after the play, consider having students present individual statements about why science and the work of scientists is important to our daily lives or how science has changed and improved our lives. Ask children to discuss these issues with parents and family at home; then hold a classroom discussion in which answers to these questions are written on the board. These answers will serve as source material for the statements you use in conjunction with the performance.

Use this play anytime you wish to let parents, other students, or the community know more about the science studies your students have completed. Charts and posters completed during regular classroom studies make useful props. Alternatively, you can simply have children make statements about what they have learned. School science fair and ecology events offer fine opportunities to round out the activities with a performance of this type.

To prepare students for use of this particular play, you will want to give children a little information about the scientists you choose to use as play characters. Make sure you let children know when the chosen scientists lived, where they lived, and a little bit about their work. For example, it is interesting for children to know that George Washington Carver developed over three hundred uses for the peanut and its plant parts.

WRITE IT

To help reinforce children's understanding of the play's scientist characters, use these scientists as a way to introduce the five-point (five sentences) report. This task can be difficult for individual second graders, but can be done successfully as a class exercise, which all students copy off

the board. Children more experienced in writing can do the five-point report based upon classroom discussion of one or more of the scientists.

Example:

George Washington Carver was a
*   scientist.*
He was born in 1864.
He taught at the Tuskegee Institute in
*   Alabama.*
He did experiments with peanuts.
He helped us a lot with his work.

By doing these simple reports, basic science words are reinforced—e.g., *scientist, experiments.*

Another, perhaps simpler, writing activity that reinforces information about what scientists generally do, is the three-in-one scientist poem. Have each student write the word *Scientists* at the top of his or her paper. Then brainstorm as a class what scientists study and do. Scientists study plants, animals, planets, fish, the ocean, weather, and so on. They do experiments, make hypotheses, and do field work. Write ideas for the work scientists do on the board. Children complete the poem by writing three things that scientists do under the heading. Have children use at least one idea about what scientists study; you might encourage older children to find out what the area of science is called (e.g., plant study is botany; planet study is astronomy).

Example:

Scientists
*   study plants*
*   do experiments*
*   read books.*

EXPLORE IT

Hold an "It's My Turn" science experiment activity. Each day for several weeks children take turns bringing in and presenting simple science experiments that they have prepared at home. Two to three science experiment presentations a day work best and take a total of twenty to thirty minutes. Have a few simple science experiment resource books available for children to review at school and borrow.

READ IT

Aliki. *A Weed Is a Flower: The Life of George Washington Carver.* Simon & Schuster, 1965.

Lepscky, Ibi. *Marie Curie.* Barron's Educational Series, 1993.

One book series that is a good source of simple experiments for children to share with classmates is the *Science Fun* series by Rose Wyler, published by Julian Messner. Some of the titles include *Science Fun with Mud and Dirt, Science Fun with Peanuts and Popcorn,* and *Science Fun with Toy Boats and Planes.*

IT'S A BIG CIRCLE

PLAYERS

TEACHER [insert a specific teacher's name, if you like]
STUDENTS 1–8   **CLOUDS 1–8**
RAINDROPS 1–13

Teacher's Notes Begin on Page 216

SCRIPT

STUDENTS *gather round one part of the stage as though look-ing through the classroom window at the rain outside.*

STUDENT 1: Wow! Look at that rain come down.

STUDENT 2 *(sadly):* I guess this means we can't go out for recess.

STUDENT 3: It's so amazing. The sky changes from blue to gray, and then all of a sudden, water falls out of it.

STUDENT 4: Yeah, it almost seems like magic to me.

TEACHER: It's not magic. It's more like geometry.

STUDENT 5: Magic or geometry. It's all the same to me. It means we can't go out to recess.

STUDENT 6: Oh, stop complaining. I don't understand, *[insert teacher's name].* How can rain be like geometry?

STUDENT 7: Yeah, geometry is about shapes like squares and circles. . . .

TEACHER *(jumping in as* STUDENT 7 *speaks):* That's what I mean. Think about a circle. What could be a bigger circle than the "water cycle" circle?

STUDENT 5: Well, I don't get it.

GEOMETRY: math study involving measurements, shapes, angles, and lines

211

STUDENT 6: Me neither.
(STUDENTS 1–4 *are talking among themselves. They seem to come up with an idea.*)

STUDENT 1: Wait a minute. We think we know what you mean.

STUDENT 3 *(pointing toward center stage):* Yes. Does the rain circle go something like this?
(*Enter* RAINDROPS 1–8.)

STUDENT 4: First, raindrops come down something like this . . .

RAINDROPS 1–4:
Plinking, tinkling
Raindrops sprinkling.

RAINDROPS 5–8:
Plopping, splashing
Raindrops crashing.

RAINDROPS 1–8 *(slowly):*
Rain water falls in a lake or an ocean
To start a process called evaporation.
(*As* RAINDROPS *finish lines, they imitate drops falling and go to seated positions at side of stage, or they can exit.*)

STUDENT 7: That's all fine. But I don't see how it's a circle. It seems more like a straight line.

STUDENT 8: And what's evaporation anyway?

TEACHER: Wait, children, let your friends finish their story.
(CLOUDS *enter.*)

STUDENT 1 (*pointing to entering* CLOUDS): So water falls to Earth as rain or snow, and then something like this happens . . .

CLOUDS 1–4: The sun warms the water so it changes shape, or
You could just say that it turns to a gas called water vapor.

CLOUDS 5–8:
As vapor, the water goes up to the sky
And cools into clouds that go drifting by.

CLOUDS 1–8:
But that's not the end of this circular tale
There's more to come, so listen well.
(CLOUDS *remain in place on stage.* RAINDROPS 9–13 *enter and stand behind some of the individual* CLOUDS.)

STUDENT 2 *(with anger):* Rain, clouds, evaporation, vapor, circles. What's really important here is that we won't get to go out for recess!

TEACHER: Now, let's be patient just a few minutes more.

STUDENT 8: I'm sorry, but I still don't see how rain is like a circle.

STUDENT 1: Okay, it's time to close the circle. You saw the rain come down, right?

STUDENTS 2, 5, 6, 7, 8: Right.

STUDENT 3: And you saw the rain evaporate up into the air and condense into clouds, right?

STUDENTS 2, 5, 6, 7, 8: Right.

STUDENT 4: Well, as the water vapor in the clouds gets cooler, and the

CIRCULAR: like a circle

CONDENSE: to shrink down

213

clouds get heavier and heavier—something like this happens. . . .

(CLOUDS *hold arms out in a curved fashion and bend knees a little so they look like they are getting heavier and heavier. Then from behind the* CLOUDS, RAINDROPS 9–13 *come out to say their lines.*)

RAINDROPS 9–11:

As the water vapor in the clouds cools more
The clouds get heavy with a watery store.

RAINDROPS 12–13:

And soon the clouds are so heavy they burst
With a storm or shower that feeds the Earth's thirst.

CLOUDS 1–8 AND RAINDROPS 9–13 *(together):*

So the water on Earth goes round and round
A more circular story could hardly be found.

STUDENT 4: So, *[insert teacher's name]*, isn't that how rain is like a circle?

TEACHER: It certainly is.

STUDENT 7: But you can also think about rain as a very hard worker.

STUDENT 8: Yes, it makes plants grow so we can have food. Without water, not one living thing on Earth could survive.

STUDENT 2: Look, it's stopped raining.

STUDENT 5: I'm glad the rain stopped working for a while. Can we go out to recess now and play?

TEACHER: While the rain was working outside, you all were working inside on this great water cycle lesson. I think you've earned your recess today. Class dismissed.

The End

SURVIVE: to outlast or live beyond some event

TEACHER'S NOTES

PERFORM IT

Costumes for this play involve everyday clothing, no-sew tunics, and crepe paper streamers. Student actors wear regular student clothing. The Teacher should wear more formal, fancy dress clothing. Clouds can wear no-sew tunics cut with rounded edges in a gray or shimmery material. The Raindrops can wear all blue with pipe cleaner necklaces onto which blue crepe paper streamers are stapled; alternatively, they can wear black and white stage clothing and hold up large, blue, posterboard drop shapes out of which face holes have been cut.

This play performance can be expanded in several ways. Follow it by singing one or two weather-themed songs or with readings or recitations of some famous short poems on weather. A good resource for such poems is the "Mostly Weather" section of *Sing a Song of Popcorn* listed in the "Read About It" section at right. Suitable poems from that collection include "Rain" by Myra Cohn Livingston, "April Rain Song" by Langston Hughes, and "Rain" by Robert Louis Stevenson.

Alternatively, you could choose to close this play by having students lead the audience in a participatory rainstorm. This is a popular activity and can be led like this: Have students spread out in front of the audience. The audience follows the sound-making activity of the student directly in front of them. Sound-making activities start with sliding hands, one-handed snapping, two-handed snapping, clapping, and then clapping and foot stomping. When the final activity is underway by all the children, it sounds like a thunderous rainstorm. Then slowly, student leaders reverse the sound-making activities, ending with hand sliding and finally silence. The storm has passed.

Performance of this play grows naturally out of curriculum studies on weather phenomena, as well as environmental discussion concerning the Earth's closed environment and the need to keep it clean.

WRITE IT

Children might enjoy creating weather similes as a play-related writing activity. The subjects to be explored include clouds, thunder, lightning, rainstorms, showers, snow, and even wind. Children compare these weather phenomena with other things with which they are familiar. Do a few as a class first. Let children choose their favorite similes to illustrate.

Example:

Lightning is as bright as a spotlight.
Thunder is as loud as a beating drum.
Rain showers are as soft as a kitten.

EXPLORE IT

The easiest way for children to experience the water cycle in class is to build a simple terrarium in a liter-sized plastic soda bottle. Each child can make one. The easiest way to make them is to cut the bottles in half with a knife. Put one to two inches of potting soil in the bottom of the bottle, sprinkle some drops of water on it, and put in a cutting of ivy or pothos or some grass or radish seeds. Tape the top half of the bottle back on with masking tape. Place in a sunny spot. Within twenty-four hours children will see the water in the soil evaporate to condense on the sides of the bottles, only to drip back down to the soil like rain. Have children log what happens with their mini-water cycles by either drawing pictures of the changes or writing in a science journal.

READ ABOUT IT

Barrett, Judy. *Cloudy with a Chance of Meatballs.* Atheneum, 1978.

de Regniers, Beatrice Schenk, Eva Moore, Mary Michaels White, and Jan Carr, sel. *Sing a Song of Popcorn: Every Child's Book of Poems.* Scholastic, 1988.

Peters, Lisa Westberg. *The Sun, the Wind and the Rain.* Henry Holt, 1988.

Simon, Seymour. *Storms.* Morrow Junior Books, 1989.

Suzuki, David. *Looking at Weather.* John Wiley & Sons, 1988.

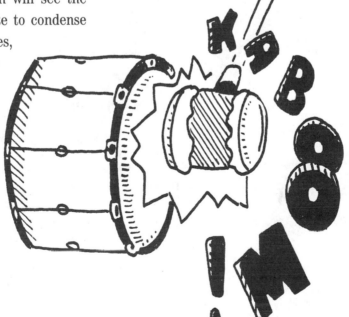

THE MACHINE

SIMPLE MACHINES IMPACT HUMAN LIFE

PLAYERS

CHILDREN 1–10	SCREW
WHEEL & AXLE	LEVER
INCLINED PLANE	WEDGE
PULLEY	MACHINE PARTS 1–14

Teacher's Notes Begin on Page 224

SCRIPT

CHILDREN *stand or sit around the stage as the play opens. Each is holding a different object. The objects can be any tools or toys that they choose; the objects are examples of the technology they are discussing as the play opens.*

CHILD 1: Isn't technology great? All these things we have help us in so many ways.

CHILD 2: And we take so many of them for granted—like our cars and bikes. Even things like spoons and toothbrushes.

CHILD 3 *(standing and looking confused):* Spoons and cars. I don't understand. What are you talking about? What exactly is "technology"?

CHILD 4: Technology is really almost anything that people make to help them do a job. It means taking really simple things and putting them together to make other things.

CHILD 5: But it's the simple things too.

CHILD 3: Like what?

CHILD 5: Well, like the six simple machines of ancient times.

CHILD 6: What are those?

(*Enter* WHEEL & AXLE.)

ANCIENT: very long ago

CHILD 1 (*pointing at the entering* WHEEL & AXLE): One is the wheel and axle. Look at all it does for us.

WHEEL & AXLE: I roll everywhere for people. I roll real cars and toy cars. I roll dollies that carry big loads. And I work and work and work inside all kinds of machines.

(WHEEL & AXLE *remains on stage but moves to side.*)

CHILD 3: Wow! I hardly ever think about how important a wheel on an axle is.

(*Enter* PULLEY.)

CHILD 2 (*pointing to entering* PULLEY): And then, there is the pulley. Look at what it does.

PULLEY: I work all around you helping to lift and move things. You use me to raise a flag and to open and close curtains. Look around, and you'll see me hard at work.

(PULLEY *remains on stage but moves to side. Enter* INCLINED PLANE.)

CHILD 4 (*pointing to entering* INCLINED PLANE): And there is the inclined plane. Look at how it helps us.

INCLINED PLANE: I don't say much, but I'm all around too. I help you move things from low places to high places. Look for me in delivery ramps and wheelchair ramps.

(INCLINED PLANE *moves to side of stage. Enter* LEVER.)

DOLLIES: platform with wheels used to carry heavy things

CHILD 5 (*pointing to entering* LEVER): Don't forget the lever. Remember how Atlas moved the Earth?

LEVER: If you want to lift up a heavy box to put something under it, you might use me.
(LEVER *moves to side of stage. Enter* WEDGE.)

CHILD 2 (*pointing to entering* WEDGE): And what about the wedge? It helps you lift many things.

WEDGE: Yes, my narrow side goes where others cannot fit, and then quietly, so quietly, I help lift the impossible.
(WEDGE *moves to side of stage.* SCREW *enters.*)

CHILD 1 (*pointing to entering* SCREW): And, finally, there is the trusty screw. I couldn't possibly count all the places you can find a screw hard at work.

SCREW: I'm your best friend for holding things together. I am much better at that job than a simple nail.
(SCREW *moves to side of stage.*)

CHILD 6: Wow! And all those simple things are part of technology?

CHILD 4: Yes. And when you put them together, you can make big, big machines.

CHILD 7: Let's build a big machine.
(*The six* SIMPLE MACHINES *now exit stage.*)

CHILD 8: How should we do that?
(CHILDREN *discuss this question among themselves.*)

ATLAS: a mythic person who had to carry the world on his shoulders

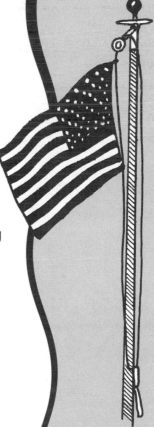

221

CHILD 9: Well, maybe we could all bring spare parts from our garages and junk drawers at home.

CHILD 8: That's fine, but what would our machine do?

(CHILDREN *discuss this question among themselves.*)

CHILD 10: I've got an idea about the kind of machine we can make. Let's get to work.

(CHILDREN 1–10 *bring in the* MACHINE PARTS *and line them up. The* CHILDREN *now create a moving machine by bringing each of the* MACHINE PARTS *to the center of the stage one at a time. This is a pantomime activity for the* MACHINE PARTS. *The first one is placed in center stage and begins a movement. Then the* CHILDREN *bring the rest of the* MACHINE PARTS *one at a time, but each new part must connect in some way with one of the other parts on stage, e.g., hand on another actor's shoulder.* MACHINE PARTS *can sit or stand or kneel. The movement they choose to make must be repeated over and over again until this part of the scene is over. One of the* CHILDREN *places a posterboard sign flat on the ground at the end of this human machine line.*)

CHILD 7: Our machine is working great!

CHILD 9: Yes, but what does it do? What's the point of technology if it doesn't produce something useful?

CHILD 10 *(picking up a piece of posterboard that says "The End" on one side and hiding that side from the audience):* But it does produce something useful.

CHILD 8: Look! It worked. It made a sign.

CHILD 6: We made a sign-making machine?

CHILD 7: A sign-making machine! That's interesting. But what does the sign say?

CHILD 10: It's a very useful sign. And I can use it right now.
(As CHILD 10 *says this, he or she walks to center stage and holds up the sign that says "The End." At this point, you can end your play, or you can use the short segment below to allow each student in your class to have at least one speaking line. To continue the play,* CHILDREN *exit stage and* MACHINE PARTS *remain.* SIMPLE MACHINES *reenter and stand to the sides of the stage.)*

[Following is the optional script segment.]

MACHINE PART 1: Thank you for coming to our play celebrating technology.

MACHINE PART 2: Before you go, we would like to share with you a few of the ways that simple machines are at work around us every day.

MACHINE PARTS 3–14: *[Here each student takes a turn stating one use of a simple machine. Students can speak about simple machines of their choice and illustrate the point with posters they make, if they choose. Sample statements might be:*

- *Four wheels on axles make the school bus go.*
- *Screws hold the handles on my bureau drawers at home.*
- *Inclined planes called ramps make buildings easier for people in wheelchairs to enter.*
- *Pulleys help the flag at city hall go up and down.]*

MACHINE PART 1: We hope you have enjoyed learning about technology and simple machines. Thank you for coming to our program.

The End

223

TEACHER'S NOTES

PERFORM IT

Children actors can wear regular school clothing as the costume for this play. The six simple machines can wear regular black and white stage clothing and enter with large posterboard signs that say in bold lettering the machine they represent. The Machine Parts are ideally all dressed in black or dark colors with no printing on shirts.

An enjoyable way to expand this play performance at the play's end is by including a segment that encourages audience participation. This can be done in one of two ways.

First, if your students do the riddle writing activity in "Write It" at right, choose five to ten riddles to read to the audience, and give the audience a chance to guess which tool is being described. Use several riddles dealing with classroom tools such as scissors and staplers.

Second, you can divide your students into groups of four to six students each and have them create pantomime versions of either the simple machines or other tools. Ask the audience to guess which tools are being pantomimed.

To best prepare children for this play, you will want to study the six simple machines mentioned in the play. Simple machines are in use around us every day, and young students enjoy identifying them in the real world. This play can be performed as an outgrowth of such curriculum or as part of a general science celebration at your school.

WRITE IT

Curriculum on simple machines and tools lends itself well to riddle writing. Children write two or three simple sentences describing how a tool works and close with "What is it?"

Example:

Q. *It opens and closes. You hold it in your hand. It cuts things. What is it?*
A. *Scissors*

Another, simpler, writing activity is to have children trace a tool on blank paper. (They can bring simple tools from home, such as wrenches, pliers, and hole punchers for this activity.) Then, on the outline of the tool, children write as many words as they can think of that describe the tool. They can write color words, shape words, texture words, and size words. They get ideas for words by looking at the tool and handling it. This builds observation and analytic skills.

224

EXPLORE IT

You might want to introduce simple machines by having children do a household survey of the machines they see around them in the different rooms of their homes. Encourage them to talk with parents about tools used frequently and how tools they use involve simple machines.

Another activity to help children really understand the operation of the simple machines is to have them build them from foil, cardboard, string, posterboard, and other pieces of clean, recyclable trash. With these materials, children make inclined planes, levers, and other simple machines. Children get very creative with this project. They will need scissors, glue, and tape to complete their machines.

Finally, a pleasant way to cap off this course of study is to have children do an art activity involving tools. An easy one is to have children trace around the tools and then use crayons and markers to turn the tool shape into a creature of some sort.

READ ABOUT IT

Horvatic, Anne. *Simple Machines,* E. P. Dutton, 1989.

Hudson, Wade. *Great Black Heroes: Five Notable Inventors,* Scholastic, 1995.

Ling, Mary, ed. *Things on Wheels.* Covent Garden Books, 1994.

The Question and Answer Books— Wheels. Lerner Publications, 1980.

Zim, Herbert S. *Machine Tools.* William Morrow Company, 1969.

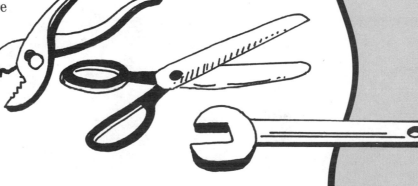

YOU ARE
INVITED TO:

_____

_____

PRESENTED BY:

_____

DATE:_____

TIME:_____

PLACE:_____

PRESENTING:

_____

BY:

_____

CHARACTERS

PLAYERS

_____ _____

_____ _____

_____ _____

_____ _____

_____ _____

_____ _____

_____ _____

CHARACTERS

_____

_____

_____

_____

_____

_____

_____

_____

_____

_____

_____

_____

PLAYERS

_____

_____

_____

_____

_____

_____

_____

_____

_____

_____

_____

_____

PROGRAM